PERU

Also by Gordon Lish

DEAR MR. CAPOTE

WHAT I KNOW SO FAR

GORDON LISH

PERU

A NOVEL

A WILLIAM ABRAHAMS BOOK

E. P. DUTTON | NEW YORK

PUBLISHED IN THE UNITED STATES
BY E. P. DUTTON, A DIVISION OF NEW AMERICAN LIBRARY,
2 PARK AVENUE, NEW YORK, N.Y. 10016

LIBRARY OF CONGRESS CATALOGING IN PUBLICATION DATA
LISH, GORDON.
PERU.
"A WILLIAM ABRAHAMS BOOK."
I. TITLE.
PS3562.I74P4   1986   813'.54   85-13015
ISBN: 0-525-24375-5

PUBLISHED SIMULTANEOUSLY IN CANADA
BY FITZHENRY & WHITESIDE LIMITED, TORONTO

COBE

DESIGNED BY MARK O'CONNOR

10 9 8 7 6 5 4 3 2 1

FIRST EDITION

My thanks to
the John Simon Guggenheim Memorial Foundation
for its expression of interest
in this undertaking.

G L

TO REGINA LISH AND TO PHILIP LISH
AND FOR DENIS DONOGHUE
AND TO STEVEN MICHAEL ADINOFF,
b. 1934, *d.* 1940

THE PROPERTY

THE CELLAR

THE ROOF

One, two, buckle my shoe.
Three, four, shut the door.
Five, six, pick up sticks.
Seven, eight, lay them straight.
Nine, ten, do it again.
Eleven, twelve, dig and delve.
Thirteen, fourteen, maids a-courting.
Fifteen, sixteen, maids in the kitchen.
Seventeen, eighteen, maids-in-waiting.
Nineteen, twenty, my plate's empty.

—MOTHER GOOSE

THE PROPERTY

I said, "But it was only just on." I said, "It was only just an instant ago when it was on." I said, "Come on, can't you tell me what it was?"

She said, "There is no one here who can do that now." She said, "Don't you know what time it is now?" She said, "I'm sorry, but this is just the night crew here, this is just the night crew now."

I said, "We had the sound off. We had to have the sound off." I said, "In all reality, how much trouble could it be, all told?"

She said, "I know." She said, "But really." She said,
"All of us would really like to be able to help you out—
but honestly, I'm honestly really sorry, the answer's going
to have to stay the way it was, it's going to have to still
be no."

I said, "No." I said, "No." I said, "We'd been packing here, my wife and I have been packing here." I said,
"Tomorrow." I said, "Starting tomorrow, our son starts
camp." I said, "You understand what I mean when I say
the boy's got to get up in the morning and leave for
camp? So the volume," I said, "don't you see what I
mean?" I said, "He's sleeping, the boy's been sleeping,
and his mother and I have had to stay up all night packing, so that's why the sound, why we had to keep it so
far down, why we had to have it almost all of the way
off." I said, "Come on." I said, "Go ahead and ask
somebody—go ahead and be a sport."

She said, "I'm sorry, sir—it is just something that
I tell you which cannot possibly be done."

I said, "We only had the picture on." I said, "Ask."
I said, "Can't you ask?" I said, "What was it?" I said,
"I just saw it when I looked up."

She said, "It's impossible. There is no one who can
answer you now. We are just the night crew now. What
you are going to have to do is call back when the regular
people come back on."

4

I said, "Yes, but I don't think you really understand me yet. I couldn't believe it. How could they show a thing like that, people doing things like that? Didn't you see it yourself? Didn't you yourself see it yourself? It was so unbelievable. I'm telling you, you have to do this for me, you have to go find somebody and ask. Because there was no way in the world for me to actually hear. You couldn't hear what it was all about. How can I sleep after this? You think people can sleep after this? Oh, come on, you must have been listening, they must have said, you must have heard, somebody there must have heard them say. One of your announcers probably, or what about an engineer?" I said, "All I am really asking for you to do is just to please do something, please go ask."

She said, "It is really out of my hands. Who do you think is here to do it for you, sir? There is no one here to do it for you, sir. It's just something which is at this hour almost all automatic, almost all a question of tape. All you have to do is call back. You call back in the morning, they'll help you out in the morning, just tell them in the morning what it was you say you saw."

I said, "Just hold it a second, just don't hang up on me for a second. Just listen for a second—no kidding, please. You have got to appreciate this, I'm going to have to find out what that was. Do you really appreciate that

5

it was just on, that it was just this instant on? Be a pal, be a friend—please just go ask someone who probably heard. Are you positive you know what I'm talking about? The news just now, it was just only instants ago and the minute right after I saw it I picked up the phone right as soon as I saw." I said, "I'm telling you, I'm really telling you, I am going to have to be up and around all night if no one's going to help me out and find out what that was."

She said, "There is nothing that can be done as of this hour. You are going to have to call back. Call first thing at nine. There will be someone here at nine. That's only almost not even a total of six more hours from now."

I said, "Even so, even so." I said, "What if a child had been looking at that? Didn't anybody first stop to consider what it was? Don't you people ever look? Does nobody ever bother to take the time?" I said, "Don't tell me these things are never checked over before you people just go ahead and put them out on the air."

She said, "It was just some footage, sir. It was just the news."

I said, "You don't understand yet—about the sound, about the sound, my boy's been just jumping out of his skin all night because of being so excited about tomorrow's being camp. So you see why he couldn't drift off? That's the reason why he couldn't drift off. The boy just couldn't drift off, and then he drifted off, but we had to stay up to get him all packed up, and so that's why my wife and I had to have the sound down, because he's got to stay down and get enough rest for the ride up to camp, but we've still been up to all hours packing him up, getting his duffel bag, getting the rest of everything for his duffel bag and his footlocker all packed up, and I just happened to be looking down into the footlocker and that's when it happened, that's when I knew the news was going to be coming on and so then I looked up." I said, "Really, it's no big deal, it won't kill you, it's not going to kill anybody—because with all of my heart I am telling you that I could just not believe what I saw." I said, "Make one single exception, tell me what it was."

She said, "I already told you, it was just some footage on the news. A prison thing—a thing in a prison— it was just some prisoners loose in a prison somewhere, some hostage thing in a prison somewhere, some kind of trouble somewhere with a prison."

I said, "Where? Where was it trouble with a prison? Which prison, where?"

"Oh," she said. "Where," she said. "So you only want to know where," she said.

I said, "Yes—that's it—I want to know where. That's right," I said, "tell me where the prison was."

"Peru," she said. She said, "They said Peru."

7

THE CELLAR

I do not remember my mother. I do not remember my father. I do not remember anyone from back before when I killed Steven Adinoff in Andy Lieblich's sandbox. What I remember is the sandbox, and anybody who had anything to do with the sandbox, or who I, in my way, as a child, thought did. Which is why I remember the nanny, and why I remember the colored man, and why I remember Miss Donnelly, who was my teacher when it was then.

I cannot tell you what I thought about the other

people, about almost all of the other people. I cannot even tell you who most of the people were, except to give you certain highlights of them when I think of them. But I don't think there is going to be anything which I can tell you about either one of Andy Lieblich's parents, or anything about what it was like inside of their place once you were actually inside of it, aside from the fact that there was a maid who always lived inside of it—not that I myself ever actually saw her other than through a screen door, or other than through a storm door, and that we ourselves, that my particular parents, that our house never had either one of those, that we never had a screen door or a storm door for any door, that the only kind of special door which our house had was the door which you went down to get into the cellar of it.

There is nothing which I will not tell you if I can think of it—Steven Adinoff is not even the half of it, Steven Adinoff is not even a smidgen of it. For instance, for instance—speaking of the cellar, for instance—I once went down to our cellar with their dog once—I once went down into our cellar with Iris Lieblich and her dog once—I went down there with her and with Sir once.

I wanted to be different things.

I wanted to be something nice.

I wanted to be just like the way he was—have hair which had the smell which his hair had, have hair which had the smell which Andy Lieblich's had, and not the smell of Kreml or of Wildroot. Or be a girl who had a place like Iris Lieblich's. Or be a lady-in-waiting and have one like a lady-in-waiting did. I mean, have a place which they could look at through gossamer, not one where you had to get off your underpants for them to see what it was.

I wanted to be Miss Donnelly's hankie, Miss Donnelly's lilac, Miss Donnelly's bodice—or just be gossamer or just be Miss Donnelly or just be Miss Donnelly when she came to a picture.

I wanted to be able to sit on the toilet and really do something. I wanted to never have to get down off of the toilet and go downstairs and have to talk to Mrs. Adinoff when she came over to my house to make my mother make me get down off of the toilet and go downstairs and have a good talk with her and let her get a good look at me and ask me the question of what kind of a boy I think it took to go ahead and kill a person.

Here is a good question for us—namely, which room of our house was it, the living room or the kitchen? And another thing—did I or didn't I have my shoes and socks off—and if I did, then did I go get them and put them back on again, or did I just pick them up and carry them back home with me—or maybe did I do neither

13

one of those two things but just instead just left them where they were, where Steven Adinoff was, plus Andy Lieblich and the nanny?

That is, if my shoes and socks had ever been actually off of me to begin with.

I was dead wrong about the colored man. The colored man didn't really have anything to do with any of it—the colored man didn't actually have the first thing to do with anything which had to do with the sandbox. It was only in my way as a child that I thought he did. I thought it was the colored man and the nanny together, that there was some way in which they were in charge of it together. However, in all reality, the colored man really didn't have anything to do with anything at the Lieblichs', except for looking out for the Lieblichs' Buick, except for whiskbrooming it out and washing it and waxing it. But in my mind it was all of it different. In my mind, the colored man was a big part of everything which went on in the sandbox—in my mind, he was just as big a part of it as the nanny herself was, even though I really knew that he actually wasn't, even though I really knew that I was just making all of this up.

But I don't know where the thought came to me from, or why I wanted it to. The colored man was just a colored man who went around and washed the cars which people had in their garages and who sometimes kept on going and gave them Simonize jobs. He was just the colored man that you told the maid to make come over if you had the money for it and actually had a car, of course.

It was just the nanny. When it came to who had the say about the sandbox, I don't think there was anybody who had as much of it as the nanny all by herself had, not probably even any of the Lieblichs.

The nanny made up all of the rules. All of the rules which went for the sandbox the nanny said were all of her own doing. Even as to the question of who was going to get permission to come over and play in it, the nanny was the only one who had the say even about this, either.

The nanny said it didn't matter what anybody else said—that it didn't matter to her what Mr. Lieblich said, or Mrs. Lieblich, or what Andy Lieblich said, or what Iris Lieblich did. The nanny said it wasn't any of them who had anything to say about who was going to get to play in the sandbox and who wasn't, or about how you were supposed to play in it if you were the one who was going to get permission to come over. The nanny said that it was all of it up to her, that the whole question of anything which had to do with the sandbox was all of it up to her, that the whole thing of the sandbox was nobody's but her own personal business and her own private affair—and that if anybody didn't like it like that, then they could go lump it, go whistle a merry tune, go fly a kite, jump in the lake, mind their own Ps and Qs, tend to their own knitting.

It wasn't the colored man at all—it was all the nanny all by herself. She was the only one who could tell you if you could come over and what time you could and when you had to clean everything up and put everything away, plus whether or not if you were playing nicely enough not to have to go home right away, plus even which were the games you could play—namely, the one of Gardener or of Farmer or of Builder, and then once you picked one, once you picked the game, she was the one who always fixed it as to who got the shovel or the hoe or the rake.

I really can't begin to remember about some of these things. What she looked like, for instance—I can't think of it. I can think of the rubberbands, her wrist, of the wristwatch.

I was a child. As such, I was a child in and of myself.

I tell you, when you live next door to someone richer, there is no end to what will enter your thoughts.

It made me crazy, I admit it.

The colored man, for instance, I had the feeling

that when I was in the sandbox that it was my job to be in it in a certain way which made me in it in place of him. However, in all actuality, I don't need anyone to tell me that the colored man didn't really know anything about me, or think anything about me, or that he probably didn't even know where I actually lived, that it was just next door to the Lieblichs and that we had to have a landlord and that I was six just like Andy Lieblich was.

The colored man, he only came there for the Buick.

If it wasn't rainy or snowy or blowy, that is. But in my memory of what it was like before we had to move away from next door to the Lieblichs, it was always weather in general like summer, like August in particular, back before the particular one when I used a toy hoe to kill a boy whose name was Steven Adinoff back in Woodmere when I was six.

It was always okay with my mother. I didn't ever have to have any permission from her—I didn't have to go get any permission from my mother to ever go play over at Andy Lieblich's or to go over there to watch the colored man wash the car. I didn't have to have her permission for anything, I don't think—except for the thing of crossing the block and therefore of going across the street, or of going on past where the Aaronsons' property came to a stop on the other side of the Lieblichs'. Not that either one of those were things that I myself would ever have asked her for, since I just took it for granted that if you went out there to those particular places, you were out there where the Christians were.

But as to the question of whether you could go out or not, it was always okay with my mother for you always to go out. I think she thought that it was good for your health—or else that she just didn't have the time to think about the question much at all. Whereas the nanny had a whole different approach to the subject of the weather—because so far as the nanny was concerned, there were all kinds of times when the outdoors was absolute poison, time after time when it did not pay to go outside, times when you were probably taking your life into your very own hands if you were stupid enough to do it, times when to get fresh air was definitely out of the question, when in all honesty and sincerity it was the better part of valor for boys to stay indoors and keep a careful vigil—especially if you yourself were actually a delicate boy, which is what the nanny said that Andy Lieblich was.

That's what I wanted.

I wanted to be a boy who was delicate like Andy Lieblich was—I wanted to be a boy who was every bit as delicate as that. That's the kind of boy I wanted to be. The kind of boy I wanted to be would be a boy who couldn't keep any fried foods down or miss his nap or not get his bath in a bathtub or ever have to get a sandwich off the kitchen counter and not be served his meat pattie when it was high time for lunch or have to have his milk without the chill off.

But even if it was nice out, even if the weather was absolutely and totally perfect out, then you still couldn't just go ahead and say that that just automatically meant that you could come over and play in the sandbox with Andy Lieblich, even if he himself, even if the nanny said that Andy Lieblich was actually going to be coming out any minute to play in it. What I mean is that there was always no end of things which might have to make the nanny make up her mind that she was just not going to be able to give you her complete and total permission at this particular juncture—namely, if it looked to her, for instance, like you were coming down with something, or that you had the first signs of some other thing, or that even if you didn't look to her like you were actually getting anything, then it maybe looked to her like this was going to be a day when you could not be trusted, like this was going to be one of those days when no matter how much you might want to promise her to the contrary, you just could not help yourself, you just could not help but not play nicely, not even if your life de-

pended on it—or maybe she just said that it was a matter of horizons, that a boy like Andy Lieblich had to
keep stretching his horizons and play the field whenever
it was humanly possible.

There were lots of times when I wasn't the one
who got to come over. There were lots of times when
the nanny had to say to me that she herself was not God,
that she alone could not just wave a wand, that there
were some things which were beyond the powers of anyone to control them, that she did not have the strength
to move heaven and earth even if that is what I and
everyone else thought she did.

But if there were other boys, if Andy Lieblich actually had over other boys, I myself never saw them—
Steven Adinoff being the sole exception, Steven Adinoff
being the first and last exception, Steven Adinoff being
the single solitary exception—but after him there were
probably lots of them.

Never more than two at a time in the sandbox,
never more than two boys at a time in the sandbox, this
was one of the nanny's strictest regulations—whereas my
idea was this—that I was the boy who lived next door
to Andy Lieblich, which gave me the first chance to be
the boy who was the second one. But what the nanny
said was that things like this were the very reason why

it had to come out just exactly the opposite—that the first shall always be last and also vice versa.

I always knew what the nanny was saying.

I always knew what everybody was saying.

I never misunderstood anything.

Even the colored man when he said things, even though the colored man almost never said actually anything.

He said chamois, for one thing.

And then there were the things which he said I should eat, the things he said which I should go home and tell my mother to get busy and start cooking for me—he had all of these different things, he had all of these different things—they were greens, they were leafy greens, a total of eight of these different kinds of leafy greens, I think, and I'll bet I could tell you the name of every last one of them, even though the colored man only told me once when in fact he finally got around to actually doing it.

I always wanted to kiss the colored man. I always felt like I was going to have to kiss the colored man. I always felt like I wasn't going to be able to help myself or stop myself or do anything to be able to keep myself from falling toward his lips and doing it.

But I didn't. I never did it. I saw how pink his

palms got, I saw how when he got them wet how pink his palms got, and I never did do it, even though there were times when his back wasn't always to me.

But he was mostly working on the Buick if he was at the Lieblichs', so his back was in general to me because, as such, he had to face the Buick, unless it was one of the times when he went into the garage for changing shirts and collecting things or for changing shirts and putting things back.

In all truth, it's true that he did not speak—it's true that the colored man mainly did not speak—but if you watched him the way I watched him, if you really kept your eye on him the way I did, then you never ended up feeling that the colored man didn't let you in on what kinds of things he thought and on all of the things of that kind. But this was probably all in my head. I was probably just making all of this up—thinking, for instance, that you could look at him doing things and then get ideas about him from that—from the way he flattened out the chamois cloth, for instance, or just folded up a rag. Even the way he shook out the Old Dutch cleanser onto the scrub brush the maid always left for him for brushing up the whitewalls, even the way the colored man did a thing like that, just tapping the side of the can with just one finger instead of actually turning it over and shaking it upside-down, even a thing as

little as that looked to me like it was something which
only the colored man did—and that if he did it for me,
if he did it in front of me, then the thought I had from
that was that the colored man specifically wanted it to
mean something to me, that it was like a statement which
the colored man had actually gone ahead and decided to
make for my own personal benefit—just things like getting the lid of the Simonize can back on again by just
pressing it down with his thumb, or things like the way
he let the water from the hose run out over the back of
the hand he used for washing the car with the sponge,
just the way he made the water come out and gush out
over the back of his hand, just things like that made me
feel that the colored man was behaving that way, was
doing things like that, only because he could tell that I
liked him to, only because he could tell that the boy who
was standing just in back of him and who was watching
him, who was watching his every move, couldn't have
been paying any closer attention to every bit of it if it
had killed him, if it had killed him—and make no mistake of it, I saw it all—the way the water streamed over
the veins which were in the back of his hand, the way
it ran out over it and then broke itself up into different
streams that just as quickly thinned out and then totally
disappeared—but then there was a fresh gush of water
and it started and ended all over again.

23

Even if he didn't actually say it, I don't think we can say that he theoretically didn't—the statement of what I stood to gain, of what kind of a future I would have as a physical being, from getting my mother to feed me the same things, the eight greens, which he once said to me he ate.

I loved watching the colored man—I tell you, I loved it with all my heart—but it wasn't anything like the love, it didn't come anywhere close to the love, which I had for the times when I was actually with Andy Lieblich in his sandbox. That was the single best feeling in the world—that was the single best thing in the whole wide world—there wasn't a sadness that I myself could ever have thought of which just being in the sandbox with Andy Lieblich could not have totally, but totally gotten rid of—especially if I stopped to think to myself, especially if right in the middle of doing something, of getting sand and filling up a pail with sand to make a haystack, for instance, or of packing it down to get it to really have the best chance of sticking together when it finally came back out, when I finally turned it over and tapped it and got it to come back out, especially if I said to myself that the colored man was taking all of this in, even if it actually happened to be a day when he wasn't even there at the Lieblichs' in the first place, or even if it was a day when he was—either way, could he see around the house from the front of the Lieblichs' property to the back of the Lieblichs' property and see me doing things? Of course not, of course not—no one had to tell me that he, that the colored man, couldn't actually in fact do that, of course—but even so, even so, it still felt to me like he could—or it felt good to me when I thought that he could, even if I really knew otherwise, even if I knew that the colored man was probably just strong and wasn't any of the other things I thought he was.

I was always the boy who was winning.

Whichever one the game was, whichever one Andy Lieblich and I were playing, whether it be Builder or Gardener or Farmer, I was always head and shoulders above Andy Lieblich when it came to who would come out winning it, who would be the one who was better at it, even if he himself always had the shovel—and make no mistake of it, even if nobody actually said it was a part of the game, even if nobody had gone ahead and said so to begin with, set it up that way to begin with, still and all, there was always a winner, there was always a winner, and the loser knew it just as much as the winner did, just as the nanny herself did, just as she herself from just sitting there did.

The chair she sat in was a slatted chair. By this I mean that it was a chair which was made out of wooden slats, like wooden boards. I think, I have the idea, that this was a pretty common kind of chair for the out-of-doors back in those particular days, which were 1938 and 1939 and 1940.

His muscles were so amazing to me—the muscles that I could see in his back when the colored man had his back to me, I could see them even though he didn't have his shirt off, even though he always had a shirt on, except for when he went into the garage to do his changing into one and then later on out of one—you could always see the colored man's muscles through his clothes because he had so many of them and such big ones.

I tell you, it was so amazing to me, it all was so amazing to me, how wide his wrists were, how thick his wrists were, or the way the back of his hand looked when he kept the water from the hose always running over it so that there always would be clean fresh water in the sponge and the dirt wouldn't get rubbed back on all over the Buick again after the colored man had gotten it all washed off.

You know what was amazing to me?

The way the colored man turned over the sponge.

It made me tremble. It made me almost tremble when the colored man lifted the sponge up off of the Buick just a small amount and then flopped it back down over on the other side—and then some of the soppiness in it flounced out, flushed out, flooded out, before he mashed his hand again back down on it.

26

Fluffed out—that's the way it looked—I am trying to really say the way all of these things looked.

You could really make a list of favorite things. You can't do it anymore, you can't do it now—but you could have done it every day of your life when you were six— Andy Lieblich and the sandbox first, the colored man after that, the colored man next, the colored man and the Buick after Andy Lieblich and the sandbox, then Miss Donnelly and the storybooks coming third.

Other things which I can think of are these—namely, seeing Iris Lieblich's place, or actually her seeing my place, Iris Lieblich seeing—and then the rest would be things I smelled and things I thought or just looking at the Lieblichs' house.

I almost forgot.

Mah-jongg, I almost forgot.

When the ladies came over to my house to play Mah-jongg with my mother—talk about favorite things, talk about favorite things—the sound of them doing it and the things they said, to me this was one of the greatest things in the world—plus the fact that it usually worked out to my getting at least one whole handful of All Sorts, which was another one of my favorite things.

Killing Steven Adinoff—there's no sense in not saying so, there's no reason not to say so—killing Steven Adinoff was one of them too.

Not that there were not times when the colored man must have seen me in the sandbox. Because it stands to reason that when he came out back to hook up the hose, or to get it back off of the spigot, he could have seen me doing different things in Andy Lieblich's sandbox, he could have looked up and seen me in the middle of doing something which not just any boy could.

The nanny, however, there was not an instant when she herself was not always there, keeping an eye out for us as regards our behavior, keeping an eye out in relation to how we were playing, to the whole question of if whether we were behaving ourselves and playing nicely enough and not letting any of the sand get out of the sandbox and get out into any of the Lieblichs' grass back there, and meanwhile keeping herself busy with the thing she always had of rolling up and down a wristful of thick rubberbands, actually rolling them up and down over her wristwatch, so that they kept rolling over on themselves, kept twisting, kept winding up too much and then untwisting, and making all of these sounds of snapping and cracking, which you could hear, which you heard going on all of the time, when you were playing something in the sandbox.

I'll tell you one of the worst things in my life. This is one of the worst things in my life—a day when the nanny said that I couldn't come over and play but one when she went ahead and changed her mind later on and said that I could actually do it—and then it started raining just a little bit after she'd said it, like just instants, just instants after she had given me her blessing—and then for the whole rest of the day, all the rest of that day after Andy Lieblich went in and the nanny went in with him, I sat down inside of our garage and kept feeling funny and out of the ordinary, as if I were in some kind of trouble and that certain things I didn't exactly know about yet were probably dangerously unfinished, lying lopsided somewhere and being dangerous, and it made me feel a terrible wildness, this strange feeling, it made me feel as if I had to feel the wildness if I was ever going to get rid of the strange feeling, which I think, to my way of thinking as a child, was the worse one, the feeling before the feeling of wildness, the feeling of incompletion and of chaos, a feeling of things getting started and of never getting them over with, of parts of it being impossible for you to ever get them totally taken care of.

In a halfway sense, I think I can say that the day I killed Steven Adinoff, that it, that that particular day—but only in this halfway sense of things which I have mentioned—was a day like that. On the other hand, now that I have said that, I think it is only fair to say that I have the feeling that I am making too much out of the thing, that I am probably not remembering my feelings so accurately.

I should be skipping the feelings and be sticking to other things, anyway. To what I remember because I actually heard it or saw it or so forth and so on—I should be sticking to things like that before things start getting too mixed up.

I heard the water going.

The whole time I was killing him, I heard the water getting out of where the colored man had it hooked up to the Lieblichs' spigot—the water he was using for the Buick, the whole time the other thing was happening, the water for the Buick was sizzling or crackling or hissing from where the fit between the hose, on the one hand, and the spigot, on the other, was a little bit loose, even though it was the colored man who had hooked it up and no one was stronger or more watchful about little things, more unbelievably careful and powerful.

Even afterwards, even when I was going home, it was still going then, the tiny hissing was, like a sizzle, like the way a frying pan with some drops of water boiling on top of the grease in it will sizzle, or make a sizzle sound.

The nanny saw it. Andy Lieblich saw it. So did Steven Adinoff himself. We all saw it. We all watched. Steven Adinoff watched just as much as anybody else.

That's the thing about it—you watch.

That's the unbelievable thing about it—that you watch it even if it's you yourself.

He watched himself get chopped up.

To me it looked like he was interested in just lying there and watching it. That you're the one who's getting it doesn't make any difference. Actually, if my own personal experience can be counted for anything, that part of it—my opinion is that that part of it is the part which just makes you all the more interested in it.

But maybe he just didn't understand what was going on anymore, what connection there was between him and the hoe, between what was happening to him and what I myself was doing with the hoe. Maybe the thing was that he was thinking of something else.

I don't know. Maybe that's what you do—you think of something else. Maybe you can't even help it, maybe you can't even stop yourself from just going ahead and thinking of something which doesn't have anything to do with the thing that's happening to you—except I myself don't think that's it, that that explains it.

But I don't know what does, what would. I can't even begin to guess—except for the fact that I think it's got something to do with a nice feeling, with having a dreamy nice sleepy and very special, very sweet new feeling.

Or else I am overdoing it or am anyway just wrong.
Maybe he just wanted to see how getting killed
looked. Maybe it didn't matter to him who was getting
killed. Because for a lot of the time he just lay there
watching instead of trying to get up and fight back, kill
me back—and then he finally did, finally did get up—
except by then he was almost dead, except by then I
think he was almost dead, even though he wasn't actually acting dead, even though he just got up and started
acting baffled and shocked instead of being sorrowful or
mad at me. But I don't think it was so much on account
of someone having almost killed him as it was on account of his realizing how he'd missed the boat on this
thing by getting distracted, by letting himself get distracted, and by not paying enough attention to it, or at
least not to the part of it which really counted, until it
was just too late and you felt silly for more or less being
the center of attention of what's going on but the last
one to be informed as to what it is all about, what it all
means. I mean, I'll bet it's like finding out that you are
the last one to get in on a secret which turns out to have
been much more about you than you ever dreamed, ever
could have conceivably dreamed, ever could have, in your
wildest imagination, thought.

To my mind, Steven Adinoff was just woolgathering and then caught himself at it and went ahead and woke himself up.

Except that it was just a gesture by then.

There were pieces of his face—there were cuts in his head.

Not that he couldn't actually get up when he tried. He got right back up on his feet again and went and got the rake again and then he walked around for a while, then he walked in and out around the sandbox for a while, stepping up to get in it and stepping down to get out of it, and meanwhile saying these different things and looking in his pockets almost all of this time, but some of it, some of the time, looking at me again and trying to get me with the rake again before I myself got ready to really buckle down to business again and he fell over again almost as soon as I really got busy and dug in.

Anybody could tell that this time it was for good. It didn't matter if you were just a six-year-old boy. Any six-year-old could have.

We just had the strength of children. We were not strong—believe you me, we really weren't. As boys in general go, or as they went in those particular times, or in that town at that particular time, that is, in the town of Woodmere, we were not what you would have called the sturdy kind of boy or the rough-and-ready kind of boy, the boy who is by nature husky in his body and hardy in his habits. You did not get muscles from the kinds of things which boys like us did, or just have them from the type of bodies which we were born with to begin with. We ourselves were not boys like that. We were actually the other kind of boy—the almost opposite kind. We did not climb things, for instance, or go to any kind of camp, or run or do things which could make you fall down, or ever lift anything which was heavy up. There was no getting, you couldn't get built up from the things we did—you couldn't get a good start at developing a good physique.

Not that I myself was anywhere near as weak or as dainty or as delicate as was Andy Lieblich himself. In all actuality, I was even on the stocky side, or at least on the solid side, by comparison with him. Even his skin, even Andy Lieblich's skin looked to me as if it wasn't strong enough to do the job of just holding him in. On the other hand, it was always nice-looking and always smelled nice—very pale and very clean. He could even get his skin dirty, Andy Lieblich could even get himself absolutely filthy and dirty from playing in the sandbox, and yet when you looked at his skin in comparison with my skin, his looked much cleaner than mine did, even

34

if I had actually gone out of my way to keep mine un-
usually clean—whereas the bad thing about having skin
like his is this—you probably could just almost touch it
with something and it would just automatically split open
or break or tear or turn black and blue or start getting
itchy.

For instance, the nanny always put citronella on
him—she had to always put citronella on him—she said
she always had to coat him with it from head to toe
even if he was only coming out for only all of five
minutes.

I thought that's what rich skin was like, that it was
skin like Andy Lieblich's.

You want to know something?

It really is.

I am a father myself now, and I can tell you that
there is no question about it—it really and truly is.

Plus the fact that it just costs more to have skin
like that—just for the plain and simple reason that you
need more things to keep it that way and to take care
of it.

A nanny, for instance—if you had skin like that,
you probably couldn't have gotten along without a nanny
to look after it, even if just to give it the time which
would be necessary if you yourself were too busy, if you,
the mother or the father of the child, were just too worn

out from other things and too busy. If I had a boy who had skin like that, I'd spend the money on it, I can tell you—Florence and I, I can tell you that we would not hesitate for one instant. Skin like that, in later life, it's a calling card, and don't you think that it isn't.

I can't tell you, I can't even begin to tell you, what kind of skin Steven Adinoff had. In all honesty and sincerity, I didn't actually pay that much attention to much other than just to his lip and to his buttons and then, later on, after it got going, to what the hoe itself was doing to him.

He was really a complete mystery to me. I hadn't even seen him before the day when I actually killed him. There were certain things about him which I never concentrated on at all. Once he picked the rake up, that was the main thing—and if you asked me what I chiefly had on my mind about him before that, then I would definitely, but definitely have to say to you that it was his lip, his lip—whereas afterwards, whereas when it was actually happening, by that time it was entirely a question of mainly three things—namely, where the trench was opening up, how his cheek looked as there was more and more of it which was coming away, and the whole general question of why he seemed to be really interested in all this, and actually doing his best to give in to it.

36

I didn't even know if he was the kind of boy who had played rough games before that, or done things which were strictly out of bounds for boys like Andy Lieblich and me. On the other hand, I really didn't know the first thing about Steven Adinoff—and, in all frankness, I still don't.

For one thing, he wasn't from the block, he wasn't from our block—and for another thing, I don't know where it was that Steven Adinoff came from—he just showed up in the Lieblichs' Buick is all I actually know— and I don't even really know that—because I didn't even really see him come in it—I was just putting two and two together when I thought that, that being on that day in August when I saw the Buick come back and then later on, after lunch, Andy Lieblich coming out with Steven Adinoff right with him—not that it matters the least little bit one way or another, how Steven Adinoff got over to Andy Lieblich's. The only point I really want to make is that he wasn't from our block, one, and that, two, when I first saw him, he was utterly brand-new to me, even though there was something about him which made me think that there was an important way in which he wasn't.

He could have been from Cedarhurst or from Hewlett or from Lynbrook or Lawrence or Inwood or from any one of the towns which were around there.

37

I just realized something—namely, that I couldn't tell you where the nanny was from, either—in the sense of where she used to live before she started living at the Lieblichs'. All I can tell you is the idea which she gave me—specifically, that it was where, that it was a place which was where all the boys were stronger boys than we were, and were Christian ones.

She said that they were wild Indians, that they were rascals, that they were imps.

She always had her uniform on, I never saw her without her uniform on—or without those rubberbands which she always had on over the wristwatch on her wrist, either. You know what I can say about the nanny which will give you the exact feeling I had about her? I can say that she always felt up close to me even when I was just thinking about her.

King of the Mountain, Hide and Seek, Tag—maybe Steven Adinoff was used to playing games like that. I don't know. Builder or Gardener or Farmer—he could have thought those were just sissy games. In all honesty and sincerity, the nanny herself, maybe even she thought that, maybe all of the times when she was sitting there in the chair there to keep an eye on us in the sandbox, maybe that's what the nanny was really thinking to herself, that we were playing a game which just a sissy would play, even though she was the one who more or less set the thing up that way herself, who said, who always said, which three games she was going to give us to pick from, and then, and who then, after we did it, after we picked, who wouldn't ever let us switch to something different no matter what.

Right this instant I could vomit from just reminding myself of how he talked—right this very instant I think I almost could, although I suppose that that's just an exaggeration from my feeling so involved in the whole question of discussing all of this, or at least from just the feeling which you have when you finally actually start.

We didn't even play games like Button, Button or London Bridge.

She said the thing she had to always watch out for with us was somebody getting too overexcited or too overheated or too worked up, and then, before you knew it, before you know it, it's all at sixes and sevens and somebody has to pay the piper. She said that that's why there had to be rules—that the reason was to keep things from getting to be at sixes and sevens.

I'll tell you one of the things she said the most.

She said, "A place for everything, and everything in its place." That's something I agreed with then—and now that I am a man of fifty years of age, all I can say is that experience has taught me to agree with it even more.

I think this was one of the reasons why Andy Lieblich was so lucky to have her. There were a lot of reasons why he was lucky to have a nanny, but this one
was one of the biggest ones—namely, the reason that the
nanny kept her eye on things for you and taught you
things which in later life could stand you in good stead,
whereas in my particular case I just had a mother to do
that and not someone extra the way Andy Lieblich did.

To be absolutely truthful with you, I personally liked
it when I had the feeling that there was a sense in which
I was the nanny's boy too—in the same way that Andy
Lieblich himself was—that is, not her flesh and blood in
the strict sense of the term, but instead her job, the thing
she was mainly supposed to be thinking about and looking out for throughout the course of the day.

Right then, right there—that's exactly it, that was
exactly it, my almost saying the livelong day, my want-
ing to say the livelong day—really feeling myself hardly
able to stop myself from saying the livelong day—it was
the same feeling, the thing with like rhyming the sounds,
or like rhyming the words.

It's amazing.

Imagine, what would I do if had a hoe in my hands?

She probably thought to herself how could boys like
this ever hurt each other? On the other hand, it was she

herself who said that boys will be boys and that you could never tell a book by its cover.

It was so quiet when I was killing him.

Aside from the sizzling of the water and her rolling them up and down, her rolling the rubberbands up and down over her wrist and her wristwatch. And make no mistake of it—I for one was listening closely, believe you me, I was all ears.

That's how I can tell you, that's how I happen to know about it—about the overall sensation of sogginess.

Here's the best way to say it—on the inside I was listening to myself, listening to the words—whereas on the outside, I was all ears, I didn't miss a peep.

Not words—but like words.

When there's time, if there's time, I'll explain.

There was never any yelling or screaming or even anybody saying "Stop!" or "Don't!" Even he himself, even Steven Adinoff himself, there wasn't one time when he said anything like that. But you know what? Now that I know what I know, I can tell you that it all makes perfect sense, perfect sense—that it's not even funny, how perfectly the whole thing fits.

You want to know what he said?

You want to hear what Steven Adinoff actually said?

He said, "You don't have to kill me."

He said, "You didn't have to kill me."

Outside of the things which he said about his Johnny Mize card, those were all of the things which Steven Adinoff actually said without a single sole exception— "You don't have to kill me," and "You didn't have to kill me," and then all these other things when he got up and was walking around and checking his pockets and stepping in and out of the sandbox—I mean, all of these other things about a baseball card, about his baseball card, the one he had when we were still waiting for the nanny to give us her decision.

There were lots of different things to hear if you are talking about just what you would have heard if you were listening to just him, then there were lots of different sounds in that specific respect—squshy ones—all told, that's the best word I can make up to describe them— squshy sounds seems to me to be the best way to state it. But, of course, that's leaving out the sounds of when, for instance, the handle of his rake banged into the handle of my hoe or somebody hit the side of the sandbox or even hit the sand itself—or hit the grass actually, the Lieblichs' lawn actually—because, if the truth be known, even in their back yard the Lieblichs had a lawn.

Here are some other thoughts that come to mind— or then let's just say just words which do.

Sluggishness and exhaustion and a kind of dragging-down feeling, the feeling of everything weighing too much and sinking, the sound of sogginess and the feeling of sogginess and of a tremendous quiet stopping and plunging, everything too heavy to move but also too heavy to stay put in one spot and stand still—all that and words, words, or just the sounds of the words—like drogue, dredge, carborundum, and torque. Do you hear what I mean? It's incredible how those ones are just the right ones—not that it hasn't taken me forever and forever to come across just the right ones—dredge, drogue, carborundum, and torque. And also inside of me, especially when I first felt the feeling of the hoe in my arms when it first actually connected so that you felt you'd connected with something solid, that's when I felt what I have to call a buzzy feeling—up deep inside of my backside—a small buzziness, small but very tingly or tingling.

Here's something I'm certain about—I had the same sound inside of me when I was looking up at Iris Lieblich looking down at me.

Ask yourself something—ask yourself if you can remember ever having a feeling like this—namely, one where you are so tired that you have to lie right down, but then the instant that you do it, then you feel that you are so tired that you have to get up again that very instant, jump up instantly that very instant, because you are even too tired to bear it, to even stand lying down for one more second.

But I think the weather had something to do with it.

It was August.

It was hot.

As such, were they having meat patties for lunch, is that what they were having for lunch? On the other hand, there is no question of the fact that the nanny said that in weather like that it was poison for someone not to eat light—that it could kill you if you weren't careful and didn't eat light.

But maybe eating something broiled was always okay. Maybe no matter what the weather was like, a nice fresh broiled meat pattie was always theoretically okay—whereas when I saw the Buick coming down past the Woodmere Academy, it was leftover meatloaf, the sandwich I had, the sandwich I was sitting there and eating, it was a sandwich of leftover meatloaf, I am absolutely positive of it.

I'll bet none of these things were ever questions which came up in Steven Adinoff's mind—the difference, for instance, between getting things broiled or fried, or having to eat a boiled frankfurter when you knew that Andy Lieblich was eating a soft-boiled egg in **an** egg cup—or a shirred or a coddled or a poached one.

44

Not that I am saying that I think that Steven Adinoff didn't know things. Far from it, in fact. Thinking back on it, reviewing the whole thing in the light of what I saw the night before Henry finally took off for camp, I would have to say that Steven Adinoff knew the deepest thing of all, just like we all would probably prove we do if we suddenly ended up in the same setup as he did with me and as those men did with each other in Peru on the roof.

It wasn't that I ever expected to go in and eat inside of there, it wasn't that I ever expected that. It wasn't that I ever even thought that I would get invited in to eat or to play inside of the Lieblichs' house, or even to just look around for a little while and see how it all was, what it all looked like, even just the things they had downstairs, even just the things downstairs inside. If there were boys who did go inside of there, boys who actually did get invited in, or who had permission to sometimes go in, then I myself do not know who they were, aside, of course, setting aside, of course, the one exception of Steven Adinoff—or also why they themselves did and I myself didn't. Unless it was a question, unless the whole thing was really just a question of who went to the Woodmere Academy and who didn't, if that in itself was the whole thing of the reason. But even if that is

45

really the case, I for one don't think I can believe that Steven Adinoff did. I mean, it's just a sense I have, or a sense which I had at the time when I killed him, which is this—that to look at him, you could just see that he wasn't Woodmere Academy material.

The time he got me in the head, on the other hand, that was interesting. I mean, in the sense in which we both of us worked together to get the rake unstuck—it was almost like a question of being well-mannered, of having good manners, him pulling up while I myself pulled down—until it finally, with the both of us doing that, came loose and came out.

Maybe I was just totally, but totally all off about the thing of Steven Adinoff versus the Woodmere Academy—maybe the whole thing he came from was actually better than I think—except I don't think his mother would have talked like she talked about being all bound up if the fact is, if the fact was that his position was anything on a par with Andy Lieblich's.

It wasn't really stuck in me that long, I don't think. But the general time span of all of this, of from when he first picked up the rake to when l either got my shoes and socks and went home or already had them on and did, plus the time of certain parts of it in particular, as to these questions, there is no way in the world where I

46

could ever come anywhere close to stating exact figures in relation to this or that particular, to how long, for instance, the rake was still stuck in my forehead until Steven Adinoff and I actually got together in the sense of teamwork and got it worked out, worked it back out.

I think one thing which we have to bear in mind is I was six—we all were six—all three of us—Steven Adinoff and Andy Lieblich and me. I mean, it's nothing like taking a boy like Henry—who's thirteen—and saying to myself, or actually asking myself, various questions about Henry when he himself was six. In all candor, frankly, I think I wouldn't have the answers to them, whereas I am almost positive that I have almost all of them in connection with my own particular case. Still and all, six is—when you stop to really think about it—all told, six is really an unbelievably long time ago for a man of any age—so that maybe with a lot of these things, I am more or less just fooling myself—but who's to say, who's to say?

All I can do is do my best.

I am trying to talk to you and make totally perfect sense.

Listen to me—it was years and years in the past. We lived in Woodmere then. We rented the house we lived in, we were just the renters of the house we lived

in, and there was a much better house next door, and
Andy Lieblich was the boy of that house, and we were
best friends.

I was friends with him.

The rest goes like this—there was his sister and
there was the dog which they had and there was the
nanny and the colored man and the Lieblichs' maid and
Mr. and Mrs. Lieblich themselves and the men who
came because of the Blue Coal and the ones who once
came because of the cesspool and the ladies who always came over for Mah-jongg, and when I went to
school, there was her, there was her—but it was still
mostly just me—still and all, it was just me—in the whole
wide world there was hardly anything but me, I was
almost—even just the sound of my corduroys when I
walked—I was almost everything there was.

And yet you know what?

The most amazing thing about this is this—I felt
so small.

My father—to me my father was just my mother
shouting out hello to him when he came home. To me
he was just what she said—I mean, just the actual words
themselves, or maybe what I mean is just the sound of
her shouting them—like this—"Phil? Phil? Is that you?
Is that you?"

I did not know what kind of work my father did,

or where my father went to do it, except that it was in New York City, that what he did was in New York City, and that it sometimes meant a lot of walking for him, and that he went to the railroad station to get there in the morning, and that he had to walk to the railroad station to get there and didn't get a ride to it along with Mr. Lieblich when Mrs. Lieblich drove Mr. Lieblich there to the station in the Buick in the morning—and then that my father had to do the same thing back the other way around again when he came back home from whatever he did to make money.

You know what else I knew about my father?

Because it's fantastic—but I still remember it—I still remember his number—the number he had for me to call him at if no one was home and something happened, if she wasn't home and something happened, if there was an emergency and I had to hurry up and call him and tell him what was what.

Imagine.

It comforts me, it comforts me.

Just imagine.

Except that I can't say what he actually could have done about it if I myself was in Woodmere and he was in New York—but not that that was something which I would have stopped to have given any thought to when I was six, yet there you go, there you go, it just made

49

me feel good right this very minute, even now it does, this very instant all of these years upon years afterwards, just knowing his number, it still makes me feel good even now that I actually know it wouldn't have done me any good then anyway and that it doesn't do me any good now, either.

You could tell that this time when he was lying back that he was lying back for good. But I don't really think that you could have said that he was actually as a practical matter dead yet. Even when I went home, even when I was on my way home, my feeling is that he still had a ways to go yet even then, but even by then I still didn't hear anybody say anything to me or scream about any of it, unless it's actually possible that people were screaming and I didn't hear them.

But I have to reject that, I have to reject that—you hear water crackling and rubberbands snapping, you certainly hear screams, make no mistake of it.

Nobody even called for the colored man to put down his things, to put his things down, and come. I mean, Steven Adinoff, he was just as quiet about it as everybody else was. That's the thing which you could probably say about the thing if you went ahead and characterized it as an overall total experience—the quietness of it, the muffledness of it—no crispness to it in any way, shape, or form. But then I have to say to myself this—that this was probably specifically in keeping with the particular weather conditions of the moment, since it was August and maybe, more than likely, it was one of those dog days which August is famous for, muggy and hazy and steamy and so on and so forth.

I don't know if I am saying this anywhere close to right—what I mean, what I meant, when I said that my father was what my mother shouted, that there was a sense in which he was the words which she shouted when she heard him at the door—what I mean is this, that to me, in my way, as a child, what she shouted at him was more actually of what my father was than anything which he in and of himself as such was—he was her, my father was my mother yelling "Phil! Phil! Is that you? Is that you?" just the way she herself was what he always yelled when my father yelled back at her "Reg!"

My father yelled, "Reg!"

Like that, just once, from downstairs, from the front door, from right after you heard his shoe, from right after you heard the one which you heard, on the linoleum, there on the linoleum floor.

The rest of it, it's just glimmers, the rest of the things about them—the way they both smelled, for one thing—that was one thing, the way they both smelled, and then her having over the ladies to play Mah-jongg with her and him always having to go to the station to get into the city to get to his work and giving me a number to call him up at in case an emergency came up.

And baths and showers, her giving me baths in the bathtub until he made me have to start taking showers.

I'll bet that all of those things probably made a very big difference to me back then, the different smells of my parents, for one thing, and these other things I've been talking about, especially her keeling over, especially the way my mother just keeled right over on me when I came home the day of the big event, especially that, the funny way my mother just went over in a way which looked to me like she was a thing made out of sticks, like this wasn't my mother falling down but was the falling down of something made out of sticks, the way she just sort of clattered down like that, my mother, right after she'd gotten back down the stairs and handed over the washcloth and sort of patted it down in my lap as if she was making sure it wasn't going to make a mess and go falling out of my lap—and then, ready or not, she just went out like a light like that, whereas him, whereas my father, I don't remember him at all from that day. He probably stayed in the city all day until I

52

myself was asleep. I don't remember him from the day of Mrs. Adinoff coming over, either, which I think was the day after. As for special things, as for remembering anything which you might call a special thing about him, there was having to have showers with him and always hearing his shoe on the floor when he came home, there was always hearing it like for the first time all over again, always hearing it there by the front door on the linoleum, that and never forgetting that I had to keep on reminding myself never to forget and make the mistake of looking anywhere in his direction whenever he had it off, whenever he had off the shoe.

What the nanny always said was, "Now give me your solemn promise, now give me your word, now give me your undivided attention and swear to me on your mother's grave that it will never be said, and said to your shame, that all was beauty here before you came. Say you swear it, say you swear it on your mother's grave. Give me your solemn promise that I will not have to send you home for not knowing how to play like a nice little fellow who knows how to play with nice things in a nice and decent way."

I always did it. I loved doing it. I loved promising her things. I loved the idea that anybody would want me to give my word about anything. I loved showing that I could be counted on to do something that I had said I would.

You want to know what was one of the greatest things in the world to me?

It was whenever the nanny gave me a chance to prove to her that I was worthy of the sandbox, that I deserved to be able to play there all of the time, that she should always feel free to give me her permission for the specific reason that I could be depended on to always do what she said and always keep my word.

Listen to me.

I was not the boy who broke the rule.

I was the boy who kept the rule, and every one of the other rules, too—I kept them better than any boy could—even a boy who was a Christian one couldn't have done any better at keeping those rules than I myself did.

We had a washtub and a wringer in the garage— we didn't have a car in there like the Lieblichs did. We didn't have a car in there of any kind, let alone the kind of car which Andy Lieblich's parents did.

I tell you, this is what the colored man knew. You know what he knew? I want you to hear what the colored man knew—which was that we both had to be people on other people's property.

54

Who could wash and wax their Buick better than he could?

Or play any of the games better than I could?

Or be better at obeying the rules?

Well, for one thing, I knew where the best sand was.

I was never in the sandbox after that. I was never in the sandbox after that, and I never saw Andy Lieblich after that, and I didn't even ever see the colored man again after that—and it was all because of the fact that we had to move to somewhere else in Woodmere.

Never saw the backs of his hands again, the back of his neck back behind his ears, his back itself—everything changed after that—the colored man and absolutely everything.

He could even nick some of the skin off of a knuckle, he could even chip a piece of his skin off—on the bumper, for instance, or on a fender, for instance, on where there was a burr in it, or a snag, something in it which was unexpected—and it actually wouldn't bleed, the place where he had caught himself, it looked to me like the colored man could just clench it up and keep it from bleeding, a cut, even a really bad one.

I never wanted to be the one who I am.

But I think I knew that it wasn't going to do me

55

any good for me to go home and start eating what he said. I think I knew that even already by then it was already too late for me to change, even if we really had any of the things which the colored man said, which I could tell from just looking at our kitchen we didn't.

We called it property. We called where you lived your property. I mean the ground itself, plus everything on it. For instance, there was the Lieblichs' property, which I think was probably the biggest property of all the different properties on the block, or which I anyhow know was bigger than our property was or than the Aaronsons' property was, and which was, from certain other standpoints—the lawn it had, for instance, and the trellises and the hedge and the arbor and the flowers—the prettiest property, the really loveliest and prettiest of all of the different properties. In all honesty, there were times when I thought it was so pretty that I just couldn't stand it to look at it—there were times when I would look at it in comparison with our property, for instance, there were times when I would look at the Lieblichs' property in comparison with our own property and I would just stand there and start to feel like I had to do something, that it was so pretty that it made you feel like you had to go ahead and do something—even just walk around on it or lie down on it or reach out and see if you could find the best place to lie down on it and hug it, actually try to hug it—the grass, the ground, the lawn—or have a dream where you could reach out your arms around it and hug the house itself.

Our property was called property too, even though we weren't actually the owners of it, even though we just were the people who were the renters of it, even though the nanny said that it was understood that we were just going to be allowed to have the use of it so long as it was all still okay with the landlord himself and we didn't break any of his rules or the things he owned—or wear anything out too much or use too much hot water or get things too dirty for him to get clean again or pester him too much, or irk him too much, about things like a new coat of paint for the ceiling of the kitchen or anywhere else.

She said that we were just temporary, that that was just how some people were, that they were just temporary people and that you never knew why this was so, but that sometimes it was because they were the kind of people who just didn't want to be tied down to anything, whereas other times it was because they were the kind of people who just could not afford to be permanent anywhere, that they just didn't have the money that you needed to really stick to things and for things to stick to you, for you to be able to build up things and get better and better in the world—and sometimes, sometimes when the nanny said all of these things, she made it sound like this was a good way to be, that it was the Christian way to be, but mainly when she said it she didn't, and I was ashamed—and then it would twist around for a while, with me making believe for a while that I myself was better than all of the rest of them were just for that very reason, just because of being ashamed, that is.

You know what she once predicted?

She said that even if I owned someday, she said that it wouldn't matter, that never in my life would I ever actually forget the fact that we were a family who rented.

In all truth, I thought it meant that he was the lord of the land—that that's what the landlord was—that he was the lord of our property just the way there was a lord of the property in Miss Donnelly's storybooks, and that the job of the ladies-in-waiting was to wait on him, to serve things to him, to bring him things on trays and to carry a cushion to him and to look pretty for him and to let him see you always standing there and waiting in gossamer.

Even when I was in the sandbox, even when my mind was just on being in the sandbox, even when that was the one thing which I was really supposed to be concentrating on, I still used to think to myself if whether

58

I would look good enough if the landlord came over, or whether, if I got too dirty, if whether he would make us pack up and move out, make my mother and father have to pack up and move out because I myself had forgotten to keep clean enough and then the landlord had come over by surprise and caught me at it, at that or at something else I didn't even know about.

Sometimes they'd call for me to come in and make myself presentable, that he was coming over and that I had to be presentable—but you know what?

The most incredible thing.

He never came.

Or if he did, I for one wasn't there for it.

I always felt I had to keep myself ready to be seen by him.

The day I killed Steven Adinoff, I think it was a day like that—I think it was a day when I had the idea that I had to keep myself ready for him, or when my mother actually said something to me which made me specifically think so. But I cannot definitely say so with any absolute assurance.

It's not important.

This isn't important, either—but I just feel like stating it—namely, that there was a sense in which I always felt like we were getting warnings, that the land-lord was always there when I wasn't there and that he was always giving us different kinds of warnings, that

59

he was always taking a look at something to see if it had reached the point where he had to go ahead and give us a warning about it, and then he did it, called my mother in when there wasn't anybody else there, and said to her that this was a warning.

The nanny used to say that she was at her wit's end, that she was fresh out of patience, that she could take only so much, that she was just flesh and blood—that, believe it or not, there was a limit to everything.

I was always trying to make the grade with everybody.

I think the reason we didn't have a dog was on account of the landlord in general, or on account of my father in particular—for the reason that he might trip over one—that my father would—but this is purest speculation, purest speculation.

We just didn't have a dog, and that is all I can say I really know about it, that is all that I can say that I really know about it.

Not that Henry has ever had one, either.

But that's because we live in an apartment, because we live in the city in an apartment, not in some house in the suburbs.

Besides, he isn't interested, anyway.

If he wanted one, if he wanted one, believe you me, he would have it, no one would deny him.

It wasn't as if we had to worry about a lawn or anything, a dog coming along and going ahead and going on it and ruining it. I mean, it wasn't like the Lieblichs' where a dog could go on it and leave a mess somewhere or ruin it.

We didn't have a lawn.

We didn't have anything even like a lawn—we didn't have anything like the way it was next door at the Lieblichs', or even like the way it was at anybody else's on the block—our property was more or less a totally, but totally different setup—more of a thing which didn't have grass as such but which was just made up of the ground itself, plus with different sections or different shapes of concrete on it, sometimes even colored concrete, sometimes red-colored or brown-colored concrete for the effect, I think, of adding decoration—circles of concrete and rectangles of concrete and certain other shapes of concrete which were specifically the shape of the area they were there for, like for around the back door or around the cellar door or around the door of the garage so that, in the case of the garage, for instance, a car could drive up into it or drive back out of it and have a smooth time of it, even though we personally didn't actually ever have a car in it, in the garage that went with the house which we rented before we had to move away to another house in Woodmere.

We had a washtub out there in it—and a clothes wringer to roll things through and squeeze the water out of them, mash a big part of the water out of the soppy wash when you picked each of the things up out of the washtub to get them ready for the clothesline.

Here again was where concrete was needed—in this case, to hold the clothesline poles up straight and run the clothesline between them—we had two places where there were round shapes of concrete in the ground with holes down in them so that you could stick the poles down in and the holes would hold them up. Not that there was always a purpose, I don't think, to all of the different places where there was some concrete all around the yard of our house, for each and every one of those different places. I have the feeling, actually, that there were some of them which were exclusively decorative, that there were some concrete places which were strictly for looks, especially the ones which were colored ones.

I'll tell you what I didn't like.

I didn't like the fact that from the Lieblichs' property, that if you stood on the Lieblichs' property, you just had to look and you could see our clothesline, whereas it didn't work vice versa, whereas the same thing didn't work vice versa, whereas you couldn't see anything which they wouldn't have liked us to if you were standing on our property and looked over at theirs. What I mean is this—what you saw when you looked from ours to theirs, it was just fine, it definitely, but definitely looked just great—you couldn't imagine how it could ever look any better even if you tried, even if you sat down and tried.

I don't know why we had concrete in our yard. The Lieblichs didn't have to have any concrete in their yard. They just had a lawn in both the front and the back. If the Lieblichs had a cesspool, then you would never have known it—if they had to have one, then you certainly couldn't have told it just by spotting a place where there was a kind of cover made up out of concrete over it and then you lifted it off and there was a steel lid underneath it and then under that, if you got that off, if you got the steel lid off, was the opening of the cesspool itself, and then there was the cesspool if you looked down into it.

I didn't know that we had one—not until the day actually dawned when I did—and then, after that, you know what I used to think to myself?

A pool of cess.

I know it didn't mean anything, but I couldn't help myself, that's what I used to think when I thought about it—that on our property there was a pool of cess and that the cess came from us, that the cess was coming from us, from something we did, from something which somebody in our house did.

In all honesty and sincerity, now that I look back on it, I think I have to say that I am glad that I never had my own dog.

I didn't like the one which they had.

I don't think you can like a dog whose name is that—whose name is Sir.

Sir.

That's really hard for me to imagine, why anybody would name a dog Sir, why even rich people would.

So many things belonged to them. I used to think that the colored man belonged to them, that he was theirs the same way the sandbox was. Of course, there is a sense in which he was, in which the colored man was. But now that I say that, then I suppose I have to also say that there is a sense in which even I was—plus my parents—that there is a sense in which we all belonged to the Lieblichs, and not just to Mr. and Mrs. Lieblich themselves but also to Andy Lieblich and Iris Lieblich and Sir.

This is probably why, I'll bet this is probably why it always felt so funny to me whenever the question of our property came up. For instance, suppose the nanny said that it was too late for Andy to come over to my property and that tomorrow was another day—or suppose the nanny asked me when was the next time going to be that the Blue Coal truck was coming over to my property so that Andy could come out to watch it—suppose the nanny said either one of those things—because I'll tell you something, I'll tell you something, things like that, any of those things, they made me feel like somebody was catching me at something, like somebody was going to catch me at something—that I was doing something terrible and I wasn't going to get away with it, that any minute they were going to get me and catch me.

I wonder if Andy Lieblich really knew one way or the other—that we were renters, I wonder if he ever knew it—and if he did, if he did, then if he just acted like he didn't just to save my feelings, just to spare my feelings—or if the idea was actually to make me feel worse.

Like someone saying that you look presentable when they know that you know you don't—and when they know that you know that they're just saying it because they have to.

Doesn't that always make you feel worse?

But maybe it could really make you feel better.

Doesn't it all depend on what they meant?

Or on what you think they did?

I could never make up my mind if they thought I should be ashamed of things for not owning anything—or if that's just what I thought.

It doesn't pay to keep thinking about a thing like this.

I tell you, there were times when I thought to myself that just Andy Lieblich by himself could make us have to move out of our house and move away even if the landlord hadn't made up his mind to make us do it yet.

But when we did have to move away, it wasn't on account of either one of them. It wasn't because of the landlord or because of Andy Lieblich.

What it was because of was Steven Adinoff, plain and simple. Not that he himself made us, of course. It was just a question of my parents deciding to go somewhere where we could start over again with a clean slate, with the slate wiped clean, with nothing against us and no hard feelings.

Whereas you know what?

Why would I want a clean slate?

Name me anything better than those particular years—even as to what finally cost me a place in the sandbox.

But that's all getting off on a tangent, after we moved and all that. I'll just say this for it, and then let it go at that—when we moved, the best car was a DeSoto, and the family which had it lived all the way up at the other end of the block.

Place is what we called your privates back then when I was six. Place was what Iris Lieblich called it when she got her underpants down off far enough and showed you where she did it when she did her siss. Or yours, yours was your place, a boy's place was a place, too— and it even went for his—for Sir's—his place once came into it, too—because she said that if it didn't, that if Sir's didn't, then she wasn't going to show me hers.

In all frankness, I didn't care that much about me seeing hers.

What I really cared about was her seeing mine—or actually was me seeing her see it.

She said, "You can look at my place if I can look at yours."

She never knew I would have liked it just as much if she just looked at mine.

She said, "You want to go over to your cellar and look?"

I always said yes whenever she asked. But it really wasn't all that many times—I am making it sound like it was a million times—when if the truth be known, it was just twice—and the second one was with him along.

I don't know what the name of their maid was. Actually, she hardly ever came up in anything. The only times I ever really got a halfway good look at her were through the screen door or through the storm door there inside of the Lieblichs' garage when she was inside at the door that you went through to go from the Lieblichs' garage on into the inside of their house—when she was waiting, when that's where the Lieblichs' maid was there waiting to get the things back from the colored man because he was through with them or where she was waiting to watch him pick them up from where she had left them on the doorstep for him—the rags and the whiskbroom and the chamois cloth and the scrub brush and the can of Old Dutch—and sometimes the cans he needed for Simonizing. That was when I saw the maid—because she was watching him, too.

Believe you me, I tried to always watch the colored man every chance I got—unless, of course, it was a time when a chance at the sandbox had come up or was going to come up and I had to get ready for it, get my thoughts ready again to play in the sandbox and be the best.

He was in there to pick the things up or to put them away—and stayed in there to change shirts.

He never told me his name.

Was it because I was a child?

Nothing's changed. I am still the boy I have been telling you about—namely, the boy who was always outdoing the rest.

I don't remember how I did it anywhere else except

in the sandbox, but I am sure that I must have also done it when I was there in Miss Donnelly's class, which was the class for the first-graders at the school where I went, which was named P.S. #5.

She was so tall and so white and had such nice dark hair.

Everything about her was everything I loved—it was all so nice—the way Miss Donnelly always smelled, for one thing, and was always saying gossamer, for another—like this—like when she would be reading to us from one of the storybooks and would say to us, "See, boys and girls?"

Not russet, not muslin, not homespun.

She would say to us, "See, boys and girls?"

She would say to us, "Gossamer—say gossamer."

We all of us said it. I said it right along with the rest. We were always saying gossamer for Miss Donnelly.

She would say to us, "Not russet, not muslin, not homespun." She would turn the storybook around, press her finger to the picture, and say, "Say gossamer. Say lady-in-waiting."

I loved saying things for Miss Donnelly.

I had the feeling that it was going to make me into a Christian to say gossamer for Miss Donnelly, or even to say anything. In all sincerity, I had the feeling that the Christians were listening to me say it whenever she asked us to say either one of those things, or other things, certain other ones which she hadn't said yet. You know what? I always had the feeling that even more important ones were coming up next.

To me, it was all just a question of its being the same thing as playing Farmer in the sandbox and making haystacks better than anybody else. What I am saying is this—that I had the feeling, that I could never get rid of the feeling, that something tremendous was always depending on it, that even maybe my life was, that my life itself did, that I was being watched and listened to by people who were going to have to make up their minds about me and decide one way or the other about it, and that everything was going to come into it—that the business of the cess would, for instance, or of how I played in the sandbox would, or if I was neat enough and put things back away all right and never spilled any of the sand out and even dusted it all off of my feet before I got back out to get my shoes and socks back on, or the thing of me having to sit and sit and never having anything much to show for it, that that was going to come into it too, that sitting on the toilet would, or it was going to be what I ate, what the food was which I ate, or how my mother cooked it for me, or something else which I had totally, but totally no control over, but they wouldn't see it that way, they would see it that I did, I did, that I actually had powers which no one knew I did, no one, you understand, but they themselves.

It's crazy, I know that it's crazy, but that is just exactly what I sometimes thought when I saw the Blue Coal truck showing up—namely, that the man who got down to shovel the coal out and the man who stayed inside were there to really see what was going to have to be decided about me—that the whole thing of the Blue Coal truck coming to deliver the coal was really just another test, just another way to check up on me in and of itself.

I am fifty years old and I know what I am saying.

Not just about this, not just about this—this is nothing so far.

I am going to tell you everything, all there is about me.

There were things which I loved with all of my heart back then. But now look—what do I love like that now? Not one single solitary thing, I can tell you, I can tell you, setting aside, of course, the question of Florence and Henry and this apartment, which, for your information, cost plenty.

We paid through the nose for it, through the nose.

What we paid for this place was a small fortune, a young fortune—what we paid for it was enough to choke a horse.

Even if you completely and totally wipe out seeing things and think only in terms of, for instance, smelling them or hearing them, then you would have to say that I was an almost totally happy little person—just smelling Miss Donnelly's hankie, for instance, or Andy Lieblich's hair, or hearing, take just hearing my corduroys on the way to school and back, or the ladies when they clicked their fingernails on the tiles, or when they tapped their fingertips on the tiles, the ladies when they came to play at my house and said things like, "One bam, two crack."

It was the only thing which kept me company when I walked to school and back.

Or hearing Iris Lieblich's underpants coming down from up around her and almost coming down all the way off, hearing the different sounds of when Iris Lieblich was getting ready for you to have your look, hearing her getting them down far enough and then getting just the one leg out of them and keeping the other leg still in—so that she could get them back on again fast enough if someone ever started to come.

But I want you to know the truth.

I liked the sound of my own coming down off more than I did the sound of hers.

Let me tell you something—Steven Adinoff had four big white buttons on his overalls.

No one ever started to come.

But we were only down there twice, and I don't think that either time it was, I don't think it was very long either one of the times which we were.

When I looked at hers, I remember saying to my-self that part of what I was seeing was the Blue Coal dust.

I probably wasn't even thinking about looking at hers so much. I was probably just waiting for her to say that it was her turn so that I could be the one, so that then I could be the one to take my own off enough and lie back down and look up at her and see her looking back down at mine.

The things you remember!

Listen to this.

I can tell you the smells of everybody—of literally everybody who counted.

Cocoa butter, the smell of cocoa butter—you could always smell the smell of cocoa butter when you got your nose up close enough to Andy Lieblich's hair—or you would smell the smell of citronella oil if you said to yourself that you were smelling his skin instead, even if your nose was almost right in his hair.

Or the smell of powder if the nanny had made him have his bath first.

Steven Adinoff, he smelled of the iron going, to me he smelled of someone ironing—whereas his mother, she just smelled of the air from outside.

As for my own particular mother, the answer in her case is the smell you get when the first puff of the cigarette has been puffed out and the smoke is mixed in with the smell of the smoke of the match, but only if the match itself was blown right out before it burned down too much and you smell the two smells together.

Guess who smelled of lilac.

Always of lilac.

My father smelled of glue.

I'm leaving out the nanny.

The colored man, he always smelled to me like what the chamois cloth smelled like when it first got sopping wet. Even before he even went near it or it got wet, I have to say that that's what the colored man smelled like to me, like the chamois cloth wet.

That was one of the biggest differences between us, the fact that he had to go inside for things and I never did—the fact that Andy Lieblich might have to go inside for the nanny to give him his tub bath or to have a nap or to be served a hot meal, whereas in my own case I didn't ever have to go back inside even when it came time to eat, even if it was time for me to eat—or even if I did go in, then I could just go in to get something and bring it back out with me and come right back out again, a snack of something or a sandwich if my mother had thought about it to put one there for me, that and a bottle of something from the icebox, some kind of drink.

The day of—that day—it was a sandwich of left-over meatloaf.

I didn't have to have a nap.

If I ever had to have one, then it was back before when I can remember it.

He was the one who made me stop having the chance to have tub baths. I think that there were a host of different reasons for it, and that not having enough hot water to go around was one of them, that somebody said that the landlord had come around and said that we were using much too much hot water for us. But I know that it wasn't just what the landlord said, that it was also what my father said, that when they were alone with each other, that when my mother and father were off by themselves with each other, that when he had her off alone with him, he told her that everybody knew that having a bath was sissyish and babyish and that it made you run the risk of coming down with something,

of getting in a draft and then of having to be sorry because you didn't have enough sense to keep from coming down with something and getting sick and having
to stay home and miss school and be in bed and have
somebody have to wait on you hand and foot when they
were already too busy to begin with, anyway.

He made me get in the shower stall with him and
start taking showers with him. He said that it was a
better idea all around, that it made more sense from
every perspective, that this was the right way to handle
it from every standpoint. But he had the wrong son for
this sort of plan. There are sons that this is probably
desirable for, I don't doubt it, I don't doubt it. It was all
wrong for me, however—it couldn't have been any worse
for a son like me, for me it was a mistake of the first
magnitude, not being allowed to have tub baths anymore
and having to get in with him when he got home from
work while he soaped himself and lathered himself and
kept doing it over and over.

However, in all other respects insofar as I can remember, there was no objection to me going my own
way so long as I made it a point not to go past the
Aaronsons' on the one side, whereas why they never
mentioned a point like this on the other side, I for one
cannot tell you or even begin to theorize. But not that it
was a question which ever even came up, given the plain

and simple fact that I didn't want to go anywhere except next door to the Lieblichs' anyway, that I never was even the least little bit desirous of any of the other alternatives, especially since I wasn't exactly certain how far you could go before you were where there were all Christians, if whether you could even cross over to the other side of the street and not start running into them.

School was a totally different matter, however, the whole thing of who was there when you got there and having to go back and forth to it. But I used to just keep my mind pinned on Miss Donnelly—lilac, hankie, bodice—plus there were my corduroys, plus there were my corduroys to always keep me company.

There wasn't someone watching me every single solitary instant—someone always telling you what to eat and when to eat and all the rest of it, baths and naps and who I myself could and couldn't have over to play.

We were friends, Andy Lieblich and I were friends—all told, we were best friends, I think, when all is said and done.

I didn't have any other friends except for him.

I had to sit there and sit there until I had something to show for it, and not flush it down until she had time to come and get a good look at it.

The nanny said that when Andy Lieblich and Iris Lieblich sat down to eat their breakfast, that one of the things which they always had to have in it was a soft-boiled egg apiece because a soft-boiled egg at breakfast was what every boy and girl needed if they were going to be able to do their business. Even a shirred or a coddled egg, she said that even a shirred or a coddled or a poached egg, she said that not even one of those eggs could do you as much good as a soft-boiled one would, even though it was still very important, even though it was absolutely essential, she said, for a child to eat them regularly if his parents wanted him to maintain good normal health and not be all bound up and constipated.

I'll tell you what else the nanny said about this.

She said that they ate theirs in egg cups, that they ate their soft-boiled eggs in their egg cups—that you had to crack around the top with a knife first and get the top of it off and then put your spoon in and scoop out all of the softest part.

That was about the only thing, I think that was about the only thing which I definitely knew that they actually had inside of there, that they had egg cups, that the Lieblichs had egg cups, although I will have to admit that I didn't really have a very good picture of what an egg cup was—I probably had the thought that it was more like a teacup, that it was shaped more like a teacup than an egg cup actually is.

But as to the inside of their house in general, as to

what it really was like in there inside of the Lieblichs'
house in general, all I can say is that I never did get any
very exact picture—my idea of what it was kept changing along with things the nanny said, and then if she
said something different, then my thoughts would take
off in a totally different direction. Just the fact that she
said she always had to make sure that he had a broiled
meat pattie for lunch, just a thing like that could get my
mind going in a certain direction and give me a picture
that would change as soon as she said something different. It was like making it up in your mind what kind
of a kitchen someone had if you knew that every day
they cooked a meat pattie in it, but then when you hear
them say something about something else, like something about always having to have their milk with the
chill off, then that's when you realize that you have to
start figuring out a totally different picture of everything, not of just their kitchen.

She said the stuff in his hair was to keep his scalp
from getting too dry and cracking. She said that if she
didn't rub a good dab of it into his scalp every day, that
then before you knew it Andy Lieblich's scalp would
start to get itchy and begin cracking.

I wonder how I smelled to him.

This is the first time it ever occurred to me to wonder how I smelled to him. But what could I have smelled

of? And was it of something different to different people?

I never thought of this before—but when I came in from being with him in the sandbox, did I smell of cocoa butter to my mother?

Nobody smells like anything to me now—not even Florence and Henry included.

I would have heard it if there had been screams. I heard the water. I heard the rubberbands. I saw everything—the big white buttons Steven Adinoff had, the blood which got on them, the dents in his hair, the dents which the hoe made in Steven Adinoff's hair, the way the hoe bent Steven Adinoff's hair down into them and how it stayed down in there in the dents, got stuck down in there in them.

Nothing is not seen, nothing is not heard.

You know what I believe?

I believe that there is no one who does not know everything—even the dumbest person.

It was no different for him. Whatever it was for me, that's exactly, I think that that is exactly what it was for him. I'll bet he even felt the same buzziness which I did—and in the very same place which I did. There is no way of knowing, I know, but I bet Steven Adinoff did.

Maybe they weren't so rich. Maybe it was just that

they had more money than we had. Maybe they didn't even have as much money as I myself, Henry and Florence and I, have right this instant—all told, all of our property, all of our holdings, plus, of course, our equity in this apartment. Except how do you account for the difference which you have when you're comparing over the distance of so many years? That and the fact that that was Woodmere, whereas this is New York City.

Manhattan actually.

Upper Fifth, upper Fifth Avenue—East Ninety-first Street, Ninety-first Street just off Fifth Avenue, to state the thing exactly—which means that a total of only eight measly blocks was all that it would have come to for me and Henry, for us to have walked it, the duffel bag and the footlocker, the whole deal.

Lackawanna 4-1810.

Amazing, just amazing—that I remember it, that to this day I still remember it.

Lackawanna 4-1810.

My God, how amazing.

Not that it all didn't all work out perfectly okay in the long run. Setting aside the question of all of the screaming and all of the carrying on, and also of the new sport coat and the necktie, the question of the new necktie as well, setting aside the question of all of that, what was it, what was it?

81

It was all a big nothing—a grand total of three Band-Aids plus nothing but some silly upset.

After all, did Henry miss a day of camp?

I don't know what kind of dog it was. It was just a dog—a boy one, a boy one. I mean, I can't say I didn't know it was a boy one, can I?

Sir.

Steven Adinoff.

Kobbe Koffi.

The names which you get stuck to you in a life.

The reason she said he wanted to see the Blue Coal truck when they came with it up to our house and then got it up close to the cellar by pulling it up all of the way up into the driveway so that they could get the coal chute out and shovel the coal out of the back of the truck down along the coal chute and reach with it through the little window into the cellar, what I would like to know is if the reason the nanny said Andy Lieblich should come over and see the Blue Coal men do all of this was because the Lieblichs themselves really had an oil burner and she just wanted to widen his horizons. Because in the years which I have been referring to, didn't people already have them, didn't people like the Lieblichs?

Just like it was people like them to also be the first ones to get the televisions.

She would get them down off enough and then I would.

And here's another thing—who picked the brand you got? Was the brand you got, was that something which you decided for yourself, or did the landlord just go ahead and pick one for you?

I actually never thought about this before—whether if Blue Coal in particular was to the question of coal in general as Buick, for instance, was to the one of automobiles. Or if whether in reality it was more like the DeSoto was.

The kind of door it was, you know the kind of door I'm talking about—the kind that they used to have down into the cellars in those days, the kind which was set into the ground outside of the house and you grabbed a handle and you lifted one side of it up and then went down some steps?

Nobody could have caught us by coming down some other steps through some other door which went down into the cellar from the inside of the house because there wasn't any other door that was inside of the house like that. The only way to go was to go down the same way we did it—not that we ever really went down there all that much. The facts are that we only went down there to look at each other twice—once with Sir, and once without. And nobody ever caught us either time—so you can stop thinking about that.

It just feels to me like someone did—but in all actuality, it's just a sensation which I have, the feeling that when we were doing it someone came down and saw what we did. It's probably just from the fact of my knowing that there is a sense in which there was someone else there, but someone only in the sense of a dog, that is.

However, I have to say that there was something just like us in him, the way he was looking and lying back and looking at you when he was letting himself be looked at by you.

You know something?

It really is your place, isn't it?

Your location, I mean.

Where you are.

Or were, at least.

It was built up a little bit with concrete on the ground all around it, which must have been for the reason of keeping rain out, snow out, mud and what have you.

I believe in God.

I do not think there is anyone who doesn't believe in God. I believe that not believing is out of the question, that it cannot be done, that it's all talk, that it's got nothing to do with anything except the sentence that says it.

84

I think I said that we ourselves did not have a dog, but I think that the Aaronsons did—Chester, if they had one, then that was his name, his name was Chester, that's the name which I would say he had.

I don't know why they would have named their dog that, why people like the Lieblichs would have gone ahead and named their dog that, how they could have picked a name which was so terrible for a dog, a name like Sir and not one like Chester. Because in every other respect, because in every other last respect, the Lieblichs didn't do things except in the way that they were done by the very best people. To me, the Lieblichs were just like the people who you saw when Miss Donnelly came to a picture and turned around the storybook—to me, the Lieblichs were almost like those particular people, like the people in the pictures, the only big difference being that they were made up, that the people in the pictures were all made up, whereas the Lieblichs were real—not people who lived in towers and turrets and you had to go over a drawbridge to get to them.

But you know what I used to sometimes see happening in dreams?

The Lieblichs coming down out of towers and out of turrets and eating the castle they lived in as they came, reaching their hands out and digging out whole handfuls of it out of the walls and actually eating them, eating whole handfuls of walls and of floors and of stairways and so on, and then me grabbing into different things too, me eating their castle too, and it tasting to me just like All Sorts—like everything it's built of is candy.

If I could understand her, then you can understand me.

Listen, for instance, to these—"Tomorrow is another day," "Rome wasn't built in a day," "Every dog has his day," "Sufficient unto the day is the evil thereof."

There was a perfect understanding between the nanny and me.

Chopped like a little trench down into the top of his head, and then saw how hair stayed stuck in it. Also a place on his face. Used a hoe. Did the whole thing with a hoe.

With a toy one.

Saw how the hair stayed down as if it was glued down like it had been dented down into it and gotten caught in the head. Whereas the thing on the roof, it didn't look like something was actually happening to that part of anybody—to anybody's head as such. It was more a question of what was going on where their clothing was—tops and bottoms made out of what looked like white stuff, like big loose pajamas made out of some kind of heavy white stuff, out of sailcloth or out of what Florence calls duck.

86

But that's not taking into account the fact of the little portable we had where we were packing Henry up—namely, that it's a perfectly good television set, but that it's just a black-and-white one and not color.

That was June.

This is August.

So guess who comes home any day now.

Like with like, it never quits—a place for everything, and everything in its place.

I acted like I didn't really know he was dead until she came and told me, but I really knew, I really did. Even before I got out, even before I put down the handle of the hoe—it was just the handle of it by then because by then the end of it was broken off of it—even before then, I knew that he was all over and done with— I knew it even before I did or didn't get my shoes and socks back on and went ahead home. But when she came and told me, for her sake, it was for her sake that I acted like I was finding it out for the first time. I finally got down off of the toilet and went down the stairs and listened to her tell it to me as if I was actually hearing something which I myself did not know.

In all candor, I can tell you why I did—which is that I just automatically knew that this was her due as a mother, that she as a mother had the right to feel that the information was all hers in and of itself.

I think that my behavior was part and parcel of my

idea of my always having to keep on presenting myself as presentable—I think that it was an outgrowth of the whole thing of that particular concept of myself as such.

She actually said it.

She said that she wanted to be the first to tell me. She actually said to me something along the lines of that—something like "Let me be the first one to tell you," and then so on and so forth, that I had killed Steven Adinoff etc., something more or less like that.

However, I think you could say that I didn't really go along with it as an absolute fact until there was some sign of it which was forthcoming from the Lieblichs.

It's just that there was a way in which things weren't so until I saw the Lieblichs do something in a way which said that something was so. Their house, for instance, my idea was that it was what a house was and that what we had, on the other hand, was something different, not a house in the sense of the idea of something which people actually lived in as such but of just something which people could go inside of when they came in from somewhere else. Oh, the way it was wood, their place, that and that it was painted white and up over the front door there was a dark green arch thing that went up and over it in front of the house, plus dark green shutters for every last window, for even the special little ones which the Lieblichs' house had in certain special places—

and I don't want to leave out that they had little screens for those little windows and also little storm windows for those little windows, and I think there were some of them up under the roof which were actually round or even oval.

But if we ourselves were best friends, then why was it that his parents didn't want to be friends with my parents? Isn't it the normal thing for the parents to be when that's what the children are? But Andy Lieblich's father, for instance, I don't think I ever heard him lean out of the car and ask my own father if he wanted to come along when Mrs. Lieblich backed the Buick out and then drove Mr. Lieblich to get the train and my own father had to walk.

We probably weren't really best friends.

We probably weren't even so close to being best friends.

He never once ever came over to my house when I asked him, and he never once asked for me ever to come over to theirs. But he always said that it was because of the nanny—whereas the nanny didn't stop Iris Lieblich, did she?

The thing is to stick to the sandbox.

It's only the sandbox which counts.

My God, my God, I keep thinking of all of the things which I haven't even begun to really think about

yet—where the good sand was, for instance—just to begin with, the whole thing of where the good sand was,
of how I always knew where the good sand was, and of
how I always turned my back to him and then dug down
for it—still feeling, me even still feeling—oh, it's amazing, it's amazing—that I can sometimes still feel it under
my fingernails, the feeling I still can sometimes get under there of the grains pushing up against them from
up under there, of granules still jammed under them,
still stuck under them, and of them pushing up my fingernails from up under them.

God love him, he's coming home almost any
day now.

I personally don't see the point of color. What you can
see in color you can see in black-and-white. You know
what I say? I say that they are going to have to come
up with a much better reason than just color itself if
they are ever going to get me to go ahead and lay out
that kind of money for just a television.

Not that Florence and I couldn't afford color if in
and of itself we wanted to. Believe you me, if you can
manage the tariff for summer camp every summer for
the past six summers, then you can certainly handle what
they get for the average color television, the price is that

measly by comparison with what they hit you up for just
for one summer of summer camp, let alone compared to
what it costs you from month to month for the mainte-
nance on a Manhattan apartment, on even a dirt-cheap
one, and this one is far from a dirt-cheap one, I can tell
you, I can tell you—because you don't get a dirt-cheap
one off upper Fifth Avenue even if the building itself is
not entirely one of the best ones.

I thought the reason which she wanted Sir along
for was because she was scared of going down into a
cellar from when she went down into ours the other
time. In all honesty and sincerity, I didn't guess even
slightly to the contrary. Who could even have dreamed
otherwise? Plus which, how is a six-year-old actually
supposed to be ready for them to have a thing which
comes out of them like that when he never had a dog
of his own?

I am going to tell you something.

I think of it, and then guess what I think of the
next instant.

I think of it, and then the next thing which I find
myself thinking of is of his lip, of his lip.

There wasn't any, there wasn't a floor as such down
there—it was just the way it was in our yard as well, it
was just packed-down dirt—except for right around the
furnace itself, where there was like a special section of

concrete instead of just the packed-down dirt all by itself.

In the sense that you got down into our cellar from going down into it from the outside of the house itself, then it seems to me that you cannot, in this particular sense, say that there was ever actually any Lieblich who was ever really inside of my house. Not that it is any different now, not that this is any different from how it is right here and now in this very building, for in-stance—namely, the fact that being neighbors, that you live next door to somebody else, doesn't necessarily mean that you have to end up socializing with each other or even theoretically acknowledging each other when you just happen to run into each other in some other context, even just downstairs in front of the building on the street.

It was a big thing for me, being the boy who lived next door to them—and it still is, it still is. When all is said and done, there is no question but that you have to see things in proportion and do your best to take the bitter with the sweet. Thanks to the Lieblichs, I was lucky enough to be given the opportunity to be exposed to things which have gone on to continue to stand me in good stead ever since. But like they say, youth is wasted on youth. It's a crime what we take for granted, every last one of us. Make no mistake of it, poverty can be a blessing—not that we were anywhere close to being ac-tually as such. We probably just weren't as well off as they were—that's probably all we were. I mean, how can children in and of themselves have any real basis for comprehending these things? Who knows but that it just could have been that God just happened to give me parents who just weren't as extravagant or as spendthrift as other parents were—maybe mine, maybe my particular parents just weren't the kind of parents who showed off the way most parents did in general.

For instance, they went to the Woodmere Academy—Andy Lieblich and Iris Lieblich went to the Woodmere Academy and I myself went, as you know, to P.S. #5—except where were you going to get a better teacher than Miss Donnelly was even at twice the price?

But I'll tell you something which still bothers me and which even to this day still gives me the whackiest feeling of things always being a little bit off, of things forever looking to you like they are just a certain amount out of line, of things never really coming together the way they're meant to and matching up exactly right. Namely, it was when Miss Donnelly read us the story of the Three Little Pigs and anybody could tell that the moral of the story was that bricks were the best thing to have your house made out of, but it was ours which was and not the Lieblichs'—whereas theirs was just made out of wood like the house of one of the foolish pigs was.

On the other hand, not to think I don't realize that

it was just a children's story about made-up houses and made-up pigs, and that no one can come along and just pick up and go from it, from the question of total make-believe, to the question of real houses for real people. Still and all, I told you the truth when I told you how it made me feel back then—and I'll tell you something else—which is that the way you felt when you were six is the way you still feel. Getting older doesn't get you any farther away from the feeling, it just gets you farther away from telling the truth about it to anybody, plus even to you yourself.

I would not have traded anything for Miss Donnelly, you could not have gotten me to trade anything for Miss Donnelly, you couldn't have paid me to take anything for Miss Donnelly, not for love or money.

The smell of the hankie she kept pinned to her bodice, the look of the finger she pressed down on the page, the sound of Miss Donnelly saying "See the lady-in-waiting? See the lady in gossamer? Say lady-in-waiting, everybody. Everybody get ready and say gossamer."

She said it was her bodice.

She talked about it like that. She put her hand on it and she called it that. She said that the place where she pinned the hankie was called her bodice.

She said, "Boys and girls, can you say bodice?"

She wore things with pleats over it, things with pleats and tucks and darts and ruffles—things like lace

94

and smocking—and she had clean flat long straight bony ghostly chalky fingers that did not taper and that had no nail polish on them and that looked like light came right through them and like they themselves could go right through things.

It felt like I was going to kiss her whenever she came close to me, like I was swooning and wasn't going to be able to stop myself, like I was just plummeting in toward her in her general direction and was going to have to fall over on her and collapse on her and have to kiss her whether I liked it or not, that it wasn't up to me anymore, that I was just woozy and a thing and overpowered by it. You know what it felt to me like whenever I was up close to Miss Donnelly and smelled the lilac smell which was always coming from her? It felt to me just like it did with the colored man, and just like it did with Andy Lieblich—it felt to me like I had to show them that I adored them, that everything depended on it, that I might die if I didn't, be lost if I didn't, be left alone, get loose, drift away, scatter, plunge, clatter off in some terrifying direction, somewhere where they weren't.

She said that she just sprinkled a dab of it on it in the morning, that she just dashed a dab of it on a hankie in the morning, that she just spattered a drop of it on it, just moistened a fresh hankie with a little spattering of it—of lilac cologne or of lilac toilet water, depending on

95

what she still had any left of from what the boys and girls of last year's first grade had had the sweetness and kindness to get their parents to get for her as a fragrance for last Christmas.

I sat in the front and looked up at her.

I heard every word which Miss Donnelly said.

She always had a different word.

Muslin.

Russet.

Homespun.

Gossamer.

You know what? I used to think that if you could just get inside of their house so that you could actually be there when Mr. Lieblich and Mrs. Lieblich were talking to each other, that what you would hear them saying would be all made up out of words like that—like muslin and russet and homespun and gossamer.

Which reminds me to tell you what Steven Adinoff talked like—because he had a harelip and he nyalked nyike nyis.

I don't know where he went to school. All I know is that it wasn't at P.S. #5. Maybe it was the Woodmere Academy, maybe he went to the Woodmere Academy, but I would definitely, but definitely doubt it, I would definitely have my doubts about it. His mother wasn't any help on this, either—she didn't shed any light on this, either—on where Steven Adinoff lived and on which school he went to—except that maybe he didn't live in Woodmere at all, or go to school in Woodmere, either—it could have been any one of the other towns I named, he could have lived in and gone to school in any one of them, plus even in one which I didn't even know about even—because I only remember Lynbrook and Lawrence and Cedarhurst and Hewlett and Inwood and Valley Stream.

Wasn't there a Valley Stream?

Or maybe what I am thinking of is of a Valley Stream Avenue.

I didn't even know what to pay attention to, I couldn't decide what to pay attention to, and I kept thinking that if I hadn't gotten off, that if she hadn't made my mother get me up off of the toilet, then I might be up there right that very instant doing something, finally getting somewhere and actually doing something.

The question is this—did we start off talking in the kitchen and then move from there to the living room, or vice versa? Or was it just her which did, or just me—and because of something she said?

Here's what it was—it was because of something I was too young for me to hear.

97

Or see.

Or just because I was a boy.

I was a child, it was a long time ago, things were totally, but totally different—I tell you, a child today could not even imagine. Henry, for instance—Henry when he was six compared to me when I was six would be like comparing the biggest opposites you could think of.

Whereas now that he is thirteen and I am fifty?

But just imagine it, just imagine it, anybody ever sending Henry out of the room because Florence wanted to say something about her bra, or her going out of the room, her actually going out of the room, her actually thinking she had to pick herself up and go from one room to another room just so that Henry wouldn't see her adjusting it, just adjusting it.

Not bra, brassiere—when I was a boy, they didn't say bra, they said brassiere—except that they never said it in front of you, except that you only heard it when you weren't supposed to.

In all honesty and sincerity, that's just what I thought about it when I heard them bidding, when they were playing Mah-jongg and I heard them bidding—I mean, I didn't know what bidding was or what any of the words were—I just knew that when they found out that I was there, they got my mother to make me not be.

One bam, two crack.

"One bam, two crack."

No one was ever actually watching to make sure I
didn't keep going after the Aaronsons', no one was ever
out there actually watching me, but I never went past
the other end of their property, anyway.

There wasn't any reason to.

I knew what Christians looked like.

There was the nanny and Miss Donnelly. I had the
nanny and Miss Donnelly to go by. Whereas as far as
the colored people went, whereas as far as the colored
man and the colored maid went, I can't even begin to
tell you why I didn't, but I myself just did not think of
them in those particular terms in general, I just did not
think of colored people as Christians or as not Christians
but just as colored people.

I realize that she was just his nanny as such, but I
have to tell you that I think there is some truth to the
statement that there were times when Andy Lieblich's
nanny also kept an eye on me.

I even sometimes used to be suspicious of something. I even sometimes used to be suspicious of the fact
that my parents used to secretly give her some money to
also keep an eye on me, that maybe there was a secret
arrangement which they had and that I was really safer
than you would think.

You know what I used to sometimes think?

I used to sometimes think that the nanny had to be
careful about always watching me so much in case some-

one spotted her at it and then told people about it and then that would wreck the whole thing of it being a secret.

She was always saying how tired she was because Andy Lieblich was such a delicate child. She was always saying that she had to watch him like a hawk, that she had to wait on him hand and foot, that she could never let him out of her sight for one instant, that she never got a moment's peace, that she never got a minute's rest, that she was dog-tired, that she was at her wit's end, that she was worn down to a frazzle with a case of nerves from it, that she was all in, done in, exhausted from running herself ragged with it, ready to drop in her tracks from worrying herself sick over it, that she was weary unto death, dead on her feet, at the end of her rope, ready to drop, irked, bored stiff, fed up. But then she would reach over for the rubberbands and start winding and unwinding them up and down her wrist over her wristwatch and start saying things about a different subject, about some other kind of thing completely different.

My mother only put out the All Sorts for when there was company.

Then somebody would say, one of the ladies would say, "Shouldn't he be outside playing?" Or "Doesn't he need the fresh air?" Or "Reggie, there aren't nice children in the neighborhood to play with?"

But I always got a handful of them first.

That is, I got a handful the size which my hand was when I was six years old.

I had nothing against him because of the harelip in particular. The only thing about the harelip was that to me it was just a totally new thing. That and the baseball card and the fact of the nanny finally saying, her finally changing her mind and giving permission, the nanny finally deciding that she was going to go ahead and make up her mind that this one time three boys in the sandbox was not going to be against the rule, these were all things which were brand-new to me, things which at the time I had to hurry up as fast as I could and get used to.

Or even just Andy Lieblich having another boy over—there was also that too.

Actually, when she said it, I thought that she was saying that what he had was a hairlip, not a harelip.

Not that I myself had ever heard of either one.

To my mind, it was filthy and disgusting, whatever it was. To my mind, it wasn't any different than what Sir's place was when she made me make it come out and then dust got stuck on it. Or what to my mind it was going to look like if you ever saw it with the shoe off of it.

To me, it was all pink and wet-looking.

And it was lifted up on one side of it.

Which made it twist all the way to his nose.

In other words, he didn't say, "You don't have to kill me," and "You didn't have to kill me." What he said was this—he said, "Nyou nyon't nyave nyoo nyill nyee," and "Nyou nyidn't nyave nyoo nyill nyee." That's what Steven Adinoff, that's actually what Steven Adinoff, that is actually what I had to hear Steven Adinoff say—plus all the rest of it, plus all of the rest of it about Nyonny Nyize.

She didn't really miss him. Maybe she was acting like she missed him, but she didn't, she didn't. It was just the next day, just the day after, but I could tell that she was already glad that he was dead. When she came over to make my mother get me to get down off of the toilet and come downstairs, she was already glad—you could tell it, you could tell it—even his own mother, especially his own mother, even a child could have looked at her and specifically told you that his own mother herself was glad that Steven Adinoff wasn't anything which she was going to have to bother with anymore, that she was trying to hide how lucky she knew she was that somebody like me had come along and gone ahead and had done what I did.

Four big white ones, two in front, two in back.

Big ones front and back.

I'll tell you something about corduroys, which is that you really do talk to them like they are a voice

which is talking to you, that you really do do it, that all
children do, even if they look you right in the face and
swear up and down to the contrary. They just have to
be alone enough, that's all it takes, being alone enough
and walking all by themselves enough and being nice
enough to know that it would be a mean thing, and
maybe even a dangerous thing, not to talk back to something which is talking to you. Not that you don't know
it's just your pants. Of course you know it's just your
pants. But what you also know is this—that there is
something which comes after the fact that they are just
your pants and that they make a noise when you move
your legs.

She said she wanted to know what I looked like,
but I can tell you this—she also wanted to know what I
talked like. You know what she found out? She found
out that I looked like a boy and talked like a boy which
she would have taken any day over the boy which she
used to have.

We both knew the truth.

We knew that I did her the biggest favor anyone
ever would.

You think I don't know about parents?

I was only six, but I knew what she thought. I
knew how she had to act, but I knew what she thought.
I even think it could be why she went ahead and said

what she said after she came back or I came back, after she had left or I had left the room—namely, to do me a favor by way of paying me back for the one which I myself had done for her.

In other words, why she said that word—that it was like a favor to me, that it was like a secret favor to me, something which the mother of Steven Adinoff could do right in front of my mother, with my own mother right there, without anybody ever knowing that she, that Steven Adinoff's mother, wasn't really and truly actually mad at me, even though she had to keep on acting like she was, as if she actually was.

Not just like glue, but also like Wildroot, or also like Kreml, depending on which one he put on when we got out of the shower.

I know mothers and fathers.

The nanny said, "This is Steven Adinoff." The nanny said, "Adinoff, now isn't it a proud name?" The nanny said, "Names come and names go, but is Adinoff one of those fly-by-night names?"

The nanny said, "Oh, I wish I had a name as grand as this lad has."

The nanny said, "Yet didn't the Lord in his infinite wisdom see fit to mark this young fellow of ours with a harelip?"

She said, "And does everybody see what I mean when I say harelip?" She said, "But is this any reason for anyone to treat Steven without every courtesy and respect?" She said, "Because God protect the boy who goes out of his way to be the least unkind or cruel to this abnormal child or to treat him like anything other than just like everybody else."

She said, "Did I have your permission to say harelip, Steven?" She said, "Because I don't want these silly little boys to be afraid of the word or to think it is something bad or to say any mean things about it or laugh at it behind your back." She said, "Now let's just be about our business and not have another word about things like harelips or anything else."

You know how I always knew which hair tonic he used?

Because I was always looking up to keep from looking down.

I thought it meant that he was born with a hair in his lip and that what you saw when you looked at him was from what the doctor had to do to it to get the hair to finally come out.

Or that the hair was actually still somewhere in there—and that what all the pink and wet was there for was this—namely, that they were just nature's way of growing something over the hair to keep it covered up.

Or maybe even of getting your attention, of getting you to look at something else.

But I tell you, there are times when nothing could get you to look somewhere else—like for instance when I looked up from the footlocker and saw the men on the roof. What I mean is not just that I myself couldn't have looked anywhere else—but that they couldn't have, either—they, the men themselves, the men on the television, the men on the roof.

Here's the proof, here's the proof—could they even look away enough to pay attention to the bullets?

My God, what amazing proof!

Henry's all for camp. Some boys, they can take it or leave it, but Henry's always been all for it right from the first time he went. Not that I can say what specifics he's so crazy about up there, which activities he likes best. All I can say is just camp things, that it's just generally things like that.

It's great, a boy as rough-and-ready as Henry is—a boy who's been all for camp for six, seven seasons now—when some boys, Florence says, would sooner eat poison than to go away to camp.

Henry just automatically loved it, was automatically a boy who was just made for camp.

Not that the one which we picked for him is anything but the best.

It's hard finding the right kind of camp. The range is tremendous—as to just the questions of quality and of program and of setting, the range is positively tremendous. But Florence handled it, Florence dealt with it—whereas it is more in my nature to keep to the wings when it comes to choosing things for Henry, to stay on the sidelines and leave the honors to Florence.

I should probably be talking to just six-year-olds. Even thirteen-year-olds, I don't think even thirteen-year-olds can really appreciate any of this anymore. Who wants to remember the way things really were? You have to really think about it and think about it to keep the things which happened from getting mixed up with the things you're always making up. Of course Andy Lieblich always got the shovel! Don't you remember how somebody always had to have the shovel? Or let's just say the first choice.

Sometimes it was so hard to decide. If you had to make your choice between the shovel and something else, if the choice you had to make was between the shovel and anything else, then it would have been an easy choice, then it would have been easy to choose—but between the hoe and the rake, what about when you have to go ahead and make a choice just between a hoe and a rake?

But I will tell you a choice which I wouldn't have had any problem with, not one single solitary problem in the least, not in the very least. However, even though it was a choice which I think it was mine by rights to make—namely, if whether we took a taxi or just walked it the morning of Henry's departure for camp—the opportunity to exercise my prerogative was denied me—and who paid the piper for it, who had to rue the day?

Not that I am saying that it was all that big of a deal—but I believe that the principle of the thing—in all honesty and candor, I think that the principle of the thing is very much to the point, if not totally and completely.

I wanted to smell of lilac and of cocoa butter.

Still do, always will.

When he started doing it, I said, "You're going to get in hot water. You're going to get in Dutch."

I'm not actually positive if that was her biggest rule. Maybe it was instead the one about the number of boys which was the biggest one. She even used to say that you couldn't even just kneel on the grass on the outside and just reach in with your pail and your hoe or your rake or what have you—she said that even that, even just reaching into the sandbox from outside of it, was definitely completely out of the question—except for the one time when she said that it wasn't.

The nanny said rules were for your own good and that she knew what was good for us. She said that the reason you had to have rules was to keep boys from

108

being flighty and fidgety. She said that if we ourselves were ever in her shoes, then that we would have the same rules which she did.

I was the best at Builder, the best at Farmer, the best at Gardener—at whichever game which Andy Lieblich told the nanny he wanted.

Take playing Farmer, for instance, take making haystacks, for instance—the way I could pack the sand down into it, the way I could pack the sand down into the pail, and then turn the pail over and give it these light taps all around on the bottom of it and then get the sand to all come out of it and stand upside-down and stay all in one piece.

But whose sandbox was it—and whose things were they—and which boy had every day for practice?

Listen to this—Andy Lieblich didn't even have to have permission to go ahead and practice. If he wanted to practice, then he just practiced. He could just automatically do it whenever he wanted, he could just walk right outside and head right for the sandbox. It was his sandbox, wasn't it?

But there was a sense in which it sometimes felt to me like it really wasn't, like it really wasn't his at all, like the sandbox was really not his sandbox but was my sandbox—just like the nanny was really my nanny and the colored man was really my colored man and the

Buick was really my Buick—that the whole thing was that there had been some kind of mix-up somewhere and that I was really the real Andy Lieblich.

In all reality, there was a sense in which I was the one who always had to have a hot lunch with a broiled meat pattie always in it and who always had to have his milk with the chill off.

He had a lawn all over, his place had lawn all around it.

They put citronella on him to keep things off of him.

He had naps and he had tub baths and I think she said a carpet, I think she once said that he had a rug, or that he had a carpet, there at their front door where linoleum was what we had.

But I have to say that it wouldn't have been the same thing, that when his father came home from the station, it wouldn't have sounded to Andy Lieblich the same way which it sounded to me when mine did—even if they themselves happened to have linoleum, even if the Lieblichs happened to have linoleum, except that I think the nanny said that they didn't.

He left almost the last day of June, whereas it's almost the end, whereas now it is almost the end of August.

I'm the same now as I was then—I always feel like

I have to be the one to do it, that it won't be done if I don't do it, that it is my job to get everything picked up and set out straight and all finished up and neat and tidy. But when it comes to things like Henry and camp, I just feel I have to leave all of that to Florence—that where it is a question of Henry and something, Florence is the one who is right on top of it.

These are questions where order and completion are a part of it, and there are questions where they aren't.

It's probably like standing and waiting for the frankfurter when it was boiling—some people being the kind of people who can just pick up and walk away while it's doing it, other people being the kind who have to stand there watching, who can't keep themselves from watching, who have the feeling that the frankfurter needs them to do it, who actually think they hear the boiling talking—the frankfurter, the water—the whole thing of it going ahead and asking you to do it.

But not asking you to.

Telling you to.

I tell you, I watched things for people.

It was the feeling I had—it was the one which I had. When I was six years old, I had the feeling that I was the one who had to watch things for people, who had to see things for people, that if I didn't, then it wouldn't be seen. I tell you, it was that way with everything—that I felt that way about everything—that I felt that I was the one who had to smell it for everybody, who had to hear it for everybody, who had to know it for everybody—that when she yelled "Phil! Phil! Is that you? Is that you?" it would have been terrible for them if I had not been there to hear it for them, plus hear it for them when he yelled back at her "Reg!" I don't mean that they said it for me—I mean that it had to go through me to get to them.

You know what I used to sometimes think?

I used to sometimes think that if I did not hear it on the linoleum in the front hall by the front door, that if I did not hear it like that when he came home from the station like that, that by the time he got up the stairs and I had to go run kiss him, that by the time I ran to kiss him hello he wouldn't have it anymore, that the big shoe would be just like the other shoe he wore, just like the regular shoe he wore, that the big one would all be gone and that he would have on one which was just a normal one in the big one's place, a shoe which wasn't so much bigger than everybody else's and which had the same shoe shape to it as all of their shoes did and which didn't look like just a sack of something soft instead. It's actually incredible, but I used to think that if I didn't pay attention to something, then it would just go away, just not be there anymore, whereas I knew that what my problem with this was always going to be was that I couldn't not do it, that I just couldn't not think of things, that I just couldn't not think of anything, that I was just like God was, that I was always going to be thinking of every single solitary thing, of even of the smallest things there were, of everything, of all of the things, of every last single thing there was, of all of them at once—of all of the grains of sand in the sandbox, for instance, of every one of those. I tell you, when I was six, I had the thought that I had to keep everything, but everything in my mind, that it was my job, that it was up to me to keep it all going by keeping it all up in my mind.

I used to feel like I had to have a bath whenever I felt a feeling of unruliness coming over me.

I used to always want to run home and wash off and go get my hair cut and be put in new clothes but always knew that I had to be outside and keep on playing and that that was my only salvation.

I wanted to look nice, smell nice, have people saying that I was being nice.

If somebody said something was spoiled or was soiled or was rancid, my first thought was it was me.

I don't think that I told you, I don't know if whether

I told you or not, that Iris Lieblich had her own sandbox
and that it was exactly the same as Andy Lieblich's was,
that the only thing which was different about it was that
it was where you couldn't see it from Andy Lieblich's
sandbox, that it was over on the other side of some
shrubbery or whatever, but that it was just as good as
his was and that she had her own friends for that one.

They both had like little roofs on top, like little
shades made out of awning, like sun shades or rain shades
which tilted so that you could aim them, plus maybe
they had a kind of fringe around the edges of them, but
I could not swear to it, little twists of cord, but I don't
think I can swear to it.

You know what the overall feeling was?

When you looked at the Lieblichs', the overall feeling you got was that it was all smoothed over and creamy
and that they never had to take care of it or do anything
to it, that it was always going to be there and be clean
and buttery and sugary and you could sit down anywhere and start eating it.

Even the nanny's chair, even though that was the
kind of thing it was, made out of slats, slatted, even that,
when you looked at it the way I looked at all of the
Lieblichs' things, even the nanny's chair actually looked
smooth and looked creamy to me even though I knew
that it really wasn't.

That was where she watched us from—she watched us from the chair.

The nanny gave me the feeling that she was more slatted than the chair was, which was probably just from the feeling which you got from looking at her in her uniform, which was so stiff from being starched that it more or less looked, that to me it looked like it was getting cracked into pieces as the day went along and as the nanny herself sat around more and more in it.

But I can't think of anything else of theirs which didn't give you a feeling of smoothness and creaminess, of things being all smoothed over and pillowy—everything from Iris Lieblich's place when she got her underpants down off of it to even the dark green shutters on all of their windows. Their things just didn't have the torn-off look which our things did. Not that our things were really in and of themselves torn off as such. What I am talking about is just the look which they had.

Or which to me they did.

I was the one who tore the head of Andy Lieblich's hoe off, but not that after that had happened to it he didn't still have the shovel and the rake to play with.

Agreed, agreed, some boys just go for showers, some boys just take to showers, my own Henry, my own son Henry, for instance, I suppose he is the shower type—whereas I myself was always the type who liked to just lie back and be in a bathtub and see the little bubbles which bubble up off of you.

I loved it.

Even if my mother didn't have the time to be with me and then be ready for me and have the towel for me when I was ready to get out, I still loved a good tub bath and the way you felt new, brand-new, when you got out.

I think that he said that the whole thing of it was a question of how much hot water we were going to be able to count on getting from our particular kind of pipes, that the landlord was going to have to do something so that this was it, this was it, so that from here on in we were going to have to just make up our minds and get used to the fact that we weren't going to be getting as much.

That it was, that taking a bath in a bathtub was babyish and sissyish and only what girls did, besides.

I am going to say something which I cannot believe that I am really going to hear myself say—which is that when I heard my father say that, that I knew my father knew.

Knew that that was what I was always thinking when I was lying there in the water soaking, knew that I was always thinking that I am doing this for him, that I am lying here in this bathtub for him, that I am get-

116

ting myself ready for him, for him to come home and find me here, that I am waiting for my father to come home from the station and come up the stairs and come see me in here—see not his son but me, his lady-in-waiting, his lady-in-waiting—clean.

We had frankfurters and beans on Saturday nights. Actually, just I did—it was just I who had them—frankfurters and beans was just what I would have myself on certain Saturday nights—but not on all of them, just on some of them—two franks and a can of Ann Page baked beans.

But probably I shouldn't have said Ann Page.

I can't swear to the name of Ann Page.

I wouldn't swear to the name Ann Page.

All I want to swear to is the fact that they weren't Heinz and that they had to keep boiling until they split open before it was okay for me to eat them—namely, that the frankfurters did, that splitting open was the sign as such that it was now okay to eat them.

That's also how you ate them—starting at the split, that is, and then peeling the skin off of them starting from that point, getting an end of skin at some point along where the split was and then pulling it off of the frankfurter until you had all of it off of it.

I don't know what they themselves had afterwards.

They ate after.

I was always upstairs in bed by the time they got around to it.

I couldn't even theorize as to their various menus. Frankly, I didn't know much about what went on in our kitchen, although I probably knew more about what went on in our kitchen than I did about any other room in our house.

My mother had a meat grinder—this there is no question but that I remember, that she had a meat grinder and did not have an egg cup.

One of the thoughts I had about the meat grinder was that there might be some way in which the pool of cess had something to do with it, but that was a thought which only lasted for a fraction of an instant—I mean, it only took a fraction of an instant to see that there couldn't conceivably have been any connection between the two things, even though what was left over in the meat grinder gave me the idea of the cesspool, or gave me the idea to think about the cesspool, despite the fact that I had never actually gone ahead and gone over to it and looked down into it to see anything down inside of it but just saw the hoses themselves going down into it and coming up out of it and smelled the smell which came up out of it.

And which I really didn't mind as much as I think I was supposed to or should have.

I even think I liked it more or less—not the idea of it, but the smell of it.

Except that I knew I shouldn't—and knew that I shouldn't ever let anyone know that I did.

Like in the way that I actually think I almost liked it when I thought of how the blood was gushing out of me like there was a hose running and the fact that my knees had actually buckled when Kobbe Koffi had clunked me one, like in the way in which I had had the same crazy automatic thought that this was secretly great, that it was shameful to think it, that I knew I should be totally ashamed of myself to even think it, but that it was wonderful, the wild thing of my knees actually buckling and of my getting my head cracked open and of me running up and down the sidewalk with all of the blood which was running out of me like that, which was running out all over me like that, and of everybody out there on the street watching it, all of those mothers out strolling with their toddlers and all of those fathers on their way to their offices and all of those kids who were waiting to get picked up for just day camps and not for a real sleep-away one like my own one was going to, like my own boy was going to go to, like our Henry was getting ready to get off to that very morning, and which he is at right now for the rest of the full eight-week season, even though they only really give you, as a factual matter, seven and a half—namely, from June twenty-ninth to August twenty-first.

Listen to this—I wanted to kiss Kobbe Koffi.

I don't know when I stopped having naps. I must have had to have naps at some point. All children have to have naps at some point. All I know is that I wasn't having naps anymore by the time which I have been talking about. However, I went to bed early—I was up in bed before they even started supper.

Here's something else—they never both split at the same time.

I used to think about the type of bed which Andy Lieblich had his naps in—and about the type of bathtub which he had his tub baths in—I used to have the whacky idea that there was some kind of a way in which they were something like the Buick, that his bathtub and bed were—but don't ask me how, I couldn't give you any specifics about it if my life depended on it. It was just that I didn't think his bed was made out of the same kind of thing which mine was, or that it was shaped the same which mine was, or something, and the same thing went for his bathtub, that when I pictured it in my mind,

I didn't picture it like ours was, up on little claw feet which had turned black and which had dug their way down through the linoleum into the wood which was under it. But on the other hand, I can't say how I did in fact picture Andy Lieblich's bathtub, except to say that whenever I tried to, what I saw wasn't a bathtub in and of itself so much as it was Mrs. Lieblich kneeling down with her arms down in the water and the nanny right behind her with a nice big towel.

You know what I thought it would look like if you saw it with the shoe off after he had taken the shoe off?

Pink and wet-looking.

Pink and wet-looking—and with no special shape to it.

Actually, when you heard it on the linoleum when he came home from the station, that's exactly what it sounded like even with the shoe on it—to me, it sounded like there was something wet down inside of it. It had a soft sound and slightly sloshy.

Whereas the sound which Steven Adinoff made was more soggy than sloshy—all told, it was less watery, even though there was actually water going, although it was only just spraying, really, just hissing where the hose wasn't fitted thoroughly tightly.

Not that I ever saw it with the shoe off of it.

Not once.

I might have looked in that general direction—like when I was in the shower with him, for instance, like when for an instant I just wasn't thinking for an instant—but I never actually saw anything in particular because even if I had forgotten for an instant where I was looking in general, I was always careful never to let my eyes get focused on anything in particular.

It wasn't just the thing of not seeing it. It was also the whole question of not seeing his place, either. It was bad enough just to be in there in the stall with him and to see all of the hair which was all over him and not to know what a lady-in-waiting was supposed to do next.

Sometimes the steam and all of the rest of it was all of it just too much for me, and I would get woozy and floppy and all set to keel over and faint, but then I wouldn't actually do it, I wouldn't actually faint—what I would do, instead what I would do was this—I would lean back away from the feeling of fainting, I would actually lean back away from the feeling of it, but I would have to lean back so hard that I would actually end up with the feeling that I was really leaning and that it was making me stand funny, that he was going to look at me and see me standing funny, that if he looked at me he would see me standing under the water at a tilt.

When we got out, he would put the Wildroot or the Kreml on—so that I would smell one or the other of those and not the gluey one.

In all reality, he wasn't anywhere near as big as the colored man was, but you thought he was when you had your clothes off.

We didn't have anything which smelled like either one of them.

Like lilac.

Or like cocoa butter.

I just automatically kept my eyes closed.

Even when I had to open them up, I had a way of not really seeing anything. But mainly, but for the most part, I kept them closed, even when I sometimes lost the little piece of soap and had to feel around to get it back again, even when I had to crouch down and put my hand down there and feel around down there—I mean, even if it meant having to put my hand down where there was like a little furry place in one certain part of the shower stall, I still didn't open my eyes up, I still didn't take a chance of doing it—I still would take having to put my hand down on the furry place over maybe having to, over my maybe having to accidentally see it without the shoe on it.

We had a meat grinder.

We had a clothes wringer.

It was not as if we did not have certain household conveniences.

Some children have more freedom than other children have.

If I wanted milk, then all I had to do to have some was just go ahead and go get it out of the icebox— whereas in the case of Andy Lieblich, the nanny said he never had it without somebody first getting the chill off of it for him—she said that drinking milk without the chill off was just like drinking poison.

Agreed, agreed, the frankfurters had to boil in the water until they were split all of the way open, but nobody even made me eat spinach when I was six years old, let alone any of the things which the colored man named when he named the eight things which he said I had to go home and get my mother to cook for me if I ever wanted to grow up and have muscles and be strong.

But I'll tell you something which every child knows.

I knew what I could grow up and be and what I couldn't—and of all the knowledge I had, I tell you, I tell you, that was the biggest knowledge of all.

The nanny said she wouldn't put anything past a mother who would feed a child frankfurters and baked beans or let him have his milk without the chill off.

Whereas the colored man said kale and collards and so on and so forth.

But I knew what the both of them were up to.

It was just like it was with Miss Donnelly, it was just like the way it was with Miss Donnelly when Miss Donnelly said, "Say gossamer." It was exactly just like that. The whole idea was to make you feel exactly just like that.

You could make them talk to you fast or you could make them talk to you slow. It all depended on which speed it was you walked at on your way to school or on your way back home from school.

It was one of the reasons why summers were lonelier—namely, because summers you didn't wear corduroys—and even if you did, then you didn't go on walks.

The colored man always did everything slow, or it always looked to me like the colored man was always doing everything slow—although the fact that it was slow or that it felt slow, that just made whatever it was all the better to watch him at. On the other hand, I don't think it was just the colored man who was slow in particular. Frankly, I think that it was grown-ups in general—that to my way of seeing things as a child, all grown-ups seemed to do things on the slow side.

I am thinking of Miss Donnelly and of the way she

turned the pages, for instance, or of how the ladies reached their fingertips out and turned each one of the tiles over, or take the nanny rolling the rubberbands up and down over her wristwatch, or the colored man flattening down the chamois cloth and pressing the last little bit of the water out, or my father coming up the stairs, or my mother coming down them.

Now when I look, you know what I see now?

I see the whole thing turned exactly the whole other way around—people my own age much too fast for me, whereas youngsters Henry's, whereas young people Henry's age, slow as molasses.

And here's proof, here's proof.

Kobbe Koffi!

How's that for proof?

It's proof positive—Kobbe Koffi with the door, Kobbe Koffi with the trunk of the taxi.

I loved to watch the colored man getting all of the things out or getting all of them put back. The only thing about it which I did not totally like was the maid watching me watch. Except that you could never really see her eyes on account of the light—so I don't know—maybe she wasn't, maybe she really wasn't—maybe when she was there just inside of the screen door or inside of the storm door, maybe what she was doing was not really looking specifically at anything.

She said that I had better take stock, that I had better face facts, that I had better take myself in hand and get a few facts straight, did I realize that life was a rude awakening?

She said that I shouldn't put all of my eggs in one basket, that I shouldn't count my chickens before they were hatched, that I shouldn't kill the goose which lays the golden egg.

You know what she said was wrong with me?

She said that I was always taking too much for granted, that I had to learn to share and share alike, that I was not a law unto myself, that I was too high and mighty for my own good, that the day would dawn when I would get my comeuppance, that butter wouldn't melt in my mouth.

Listen to me—I knew what she meant.

He held the sponge in one hand and the hose in the other. The hand which held the sponge, the hand which held the sponge, he ran the water over the back of that hand with the hand which held the hose.

I didn't even wash the shoes off. I just used the Vernax on them right the way they were. But the sport coat and the necktie, they were totally, but totally ruined.

They were just no good anymore, those things, the

new things, the things which I'd gone ahead and gotten for just that morning, for the morning in question—plus the shirt, the pants, my socks—all of it, every bit of it, all a total loss. The only thing that was any good anymore was just the shoes which I had had on. But that's thanks to Vernax, that I can thank Vernax for.

I just put it on them.

I didn't even wash the blood off as such.

Actually, if the facts be known, they look even better than they did before it happened.

But just think of it, just think of it—even my socks, my socks—that's how it was just pouring out of me. I'm telling you, I was soaked, literally soaked, literally drenched—I was even walking in it, actually walking in it, it was down inside my shoes.

But what did the whole thing come to when they got me all cleaned up?

Three Band-Aids, a grand total of three Band-Aids, two of which didn't even have anything to do with the blood itself as such.

Incredible.

Absolutely and totally incredible.

And I thought that was it.

My God, my God.

Oh, dear God.

But I tell you, I was so scared.

I don't think it was of death.

I think the thing I was actually the most scared of was of Henry missing the bus up to camp, of that and something else.

He just fell over.

It amazed me, it was amazing to me, the way someone else could just fall over. It was really an amazing thing for me to see, how you could just go ahead and do something and then someone else just falls over just because you yourself actually went ahead and did it to them.

I think I should mention this—that we didn't have screen windows or storm windows or setups of that kind for our doors.

I think I should mention this—that when I think back to the time which I have been talking about, it's always hot, the weather's always summer.

On the other hand, it is summer now.

This might be the cause of it.

When all is said and done, anything could be the cause of it in and of itself.

It wasn't always the hoe which I hit him with. A certain part of the time it was just the handle of the hoe

that I did it with, the reason for this being that the other
part broke off, that at a certain point it just broke off.

She said that we were always getting overexcited or
overheated or all worked up and carried away.

She said that moderation was always the best policy.

She said that slow and easy won the race.

She said that it was better to be safe than sorry.

I never didn't obey her. I just always automatically
did what the nanny said. I had the idea that if I didn't
do it, then that she would go tell the Christians.

You know what I used to think?

I used to think that when the day was all over and
done with, that she used to go somewhere down past
the Aaronsons' and talk to them, report to them, turn
over to them a kind of report for the day—that the
Christians were waiting for her down past the Aaronsons' property for the nanny to come tell them what she
said all of us did.

You know what else?

I had the thought that nobody else knew about it—
that I myself was the only one who knew anything about
it. But in all actuality, I think that I had the same thought
about not just the nanny herself but also about everyone
else—namely, that there was a secret which they had
and that I was the only one who knew that they had

one, except that the strangest thing about it was that I didn't know what it was.

Or at least not in so many words.

Where Miss Donnelly put her finger, for instance, or how he ran the water over the back of his hand, or the looks they gave our house when they drove the truck up and got out to shovel in the Blue Coal.

Everything made me tired.

Everything sapped my strength.

Every time I finished playing in the sandbox, there was no more strength left in me to ever play again, there was no more strength left in me to ever be the best again, and I would think to myself, I would have the thought to myself, that there will never be any more of anything left in me again, even to live with, even just to live with, let alone to play.

No boy made haystacks any better than I did!

Didn't she ever hear it when I said gossamer better than the rest?

I want to say something, I have to say something— it doesn't matter what you say.

I used to wait for her to come take me by the hand. I used to wait for all of them to come take me by the hand.

You know the question I had?

Here is the question I had.

When was the best boy going to go ahead and get permission to go to the Woodmere Academy?

Or get to have a ride in the Buick?

Here is how it felt when his mother came over—it felt the same to me as it felt when I looked up and saw Iris Lieblich looking down at me. It felt the same to me as when it was my turn. It felt good.

If the truth be known, I think it felt good to her, too.

Florence says that mineral oil on a regular basis, she says that always depending so much on mineral oil, she says that she read that too great a reliance on mineral oil can result in intestinal damage.

In loss of muscle tone or something.

But that doesn't sound right, does it?

Atrophy—some kind of atrophy.

Some kind of function.

Or dysfunction.

Whereas all I can say is thank God that Henry does not take after me.

They said for me to go inside and ask her what was happening—they said that if I didn't know what was happening, then that I should go inside and ask her what was happening—they said that they themselves were not going to have the time to sit me down and explain it to me, but that if I went inside, that then my mother would. But I didn't think that I could do that. I didn't think that I should do that. I thought that it might hurt her feelings if I did that. I actually even thought that maybe it was why they were there in the first place, that this was why the men were there at our house just to begin with, that the whole thing of it of them being there—the hoses and the top off and the smell of it all over everywhere—was just to hurt her feelings, that the landlord had sent them over to our house to hurt my parents' feelings—that it was because of the hot water, that it was all because of the hot water, that it was on account of him getting angry with them for always asking him to give us more of it—the thought I had was that they must have always been asking him to give us more of it because I wanted for there to be more of it, because they knew that I wanted for there to be more of it, because if there was more of it, because if there was more of it when we needed to have hot water for something, then would I have to keep on getting into the shower stall with him? Would I have to wait for him to come home from the station and come up the stairs and then have to get into the shower stall with him?

I never asked anyone about the cesspool. I decided never to ask anyone about the cesspool. I decided all

about it without ever asking anyone. What I decided
was that it didn't work for the landlord as much as he
planned for it to because I was there and I liked the
smell of it, whereas you weren't supposed to, you weren't
supposed to.

I decided that it was because of me that we came
out ahead of the landlord.

But here is another thing which I decided—namely,
that the cess came off of him from when he took a shower,
that the water and the soap washed it off of him where
the shoe was and then it went down the drain and into
the pipe and ended up out front in the front yard down
in the ground in a big pool of it.

I think Steven Adinoff's mother wanted to do
something nice for me. I think that she wanted to, but
that she didn't know how to. I think that the whole
thing was a question of her being afraid of getting caught
at it if she tried to—and so that that's why, that that
was the reason why she made up the business about how
her brassiere was. In all honesty and sincerity, that's why
I think that she did it—that it was a secret way of saying
thank you, that it was a way of her saying it so secretly
that only I myself would know but my mother wouldn't.

I am not wrong about this.

I know what I am saying.

Take it from me, you only have to be a parent.

She owed me.

She was thanking me. It was the secret which we had between us—that she was thanking me, that she had to thank me, that this was going to be the one time which she was ever going to get to go ahead and say thank you to me.

Think of it.

I wasn't entitled?

Up until I had come along, up until I came along, you know the kind of boy she had? Here is the kind of boy she had—she had a boy who nyalked nyike nyis.

I had it coming, something nice from her—something like hankie, like gossamer, like bodice.

I tell you, don't tell me about parents!

It feels like sand sometimes, it feels like grains of sand sometimes, like granules of sand, like the pressure of sand, it sometimes feels to me like there's this grit, these grains of it, pushing up from under my fingernails, like there's still some sand which is stuck up under there, that special sand I specifically dug way down in the corners for, to get the sand for haystacks which would always come out perfect.

Because that was the thing about that sand as opposed to the regular sand, as opposed to the sand which Andy Lieblich got off of the top of the sand and which he put into his pail—namely, that the special sand stuck together like that—and that it also stuck to you, too, of course.

You know what it was like?

It was like a secret between me and the sandbox.

There were probably only two hoses—in all reality, there probably were only, all told, just a total of two hoses—but to me it looked like there were hoses everywhere, and not the kind the colored man had for when he went ahead and did the Buick, but big white thick ones instead, big thick hoses which were made out of like something like canvas.

What I mean is that they were just automatically there, that I just came home from school and that they were just there, that there they were and that no one had told me to get ready for them, that in the morning when I went to school, that no one had told me anything beforehand, and so I just came home like that and then there they were, that I had just been walking along like that and just looked up, and that no one, not my mother, not my father, not anyone in all the whole wide world, had said anything to me first, had told me to get ready for it first, had said to me that they were going to be there like that when I got home from school, that they were going to be there in the front yard like that, hoses, hoses of a kind which I myself had never had any experience with before, big thick white ones going down into the ground where there had been a round lid of concrete moved off the top of it to make way, hoses going down, or hoses coming up, and the noise of something pumping, and people out to watch, maids from different houses, from houses past the Aaronsons' house, from houses where I didn't even know the names of the people.

I felt like my corduroys had been in on it, like even my own corduroys had been in on it and had gone back on me, gone against me, had been in on it and kept it secret from me, that it was my property and that I had a right to be ready for it, that wasn't I the one who knew all of the secrets and was supposed to be ready for everything, even for the Christians, even for the Christians?

But then when I got to like the smell of it, then it was all okay again—because I knew what the truth was, which was that you weren't supposed to like it, whereas if I did, whereas if I myself did, then I was back to being the best at things again—the best at everything from playing in the sandbox to saying gossamer.

My attention was on the packing, my attention was completely and totally on the packing, which could account for, which could actually have been a big contributing factor, which actually probably accounts for a lot of the impact—just looking up from something you're so completely absorbed in, just being taken so totally by surprise by something—that plus just being so tired just to begin with, so worn out in the first place, so totally exhausted from just the lateness of the hour and from still trying to get all of that stuff jammed down into the duffel bag and shoved down into the footlocker and from even still doing the inventory when it should have been done long ago, from just trying to count undershorts and T-shirts, if you can imagine it, if you really can imagine it, there at that hour of the night, or really at that of the morning, actually.

I don't know if I have said this yet, but it is a top-rated camp.

You know what else?

Not to think it doesn't have a tuition to go along with it!

But as for what happened the morning of, call it a case of distraction, pure and simple.

I just wasn't paying attention.

I was just acting like an idiot, like every other city idiot—overtaxed, overtired, overexcited—a city husband, a city father, a man overburdened, plain and simple, a man who has had too much.

My God, just to be able to concentrate on something the way you could do it when you were six—just to be able to put all of your mind into it and all of your heart into it—and your whole body, your whole body— just to be able to do that with anything again just for one single solitary instant.

But you know what?

I couldn't even get all of my attention on myself even when I thought that my head, even when then and there in that first whacky instant when I was totally certain of it, convinced, convinced that my head was bashed in, cracked open, smashed, totally smashed.

Even then I was somewhere else.

Dot!

When they played Mah-jongg, when they said bam this, bam that, crack this, crack that, they also said dot, they also said dot—something like "One bam, two crack, three dot."

I made a fool of myself. I made a complete fool of myself. And I almost made Henry miss his bus.

Plus which I cost us plenty in special freight charges getting the stuff up to him on an overnight truck.

It was really just total lunacy from start to finish— from one end to the other, it really was. I tell you, the only thing which was missing from it, the only thing which you could say was left out of it was the banana peel—that and the cane and the top hat.

It was slapstick, it was farce.

You know what it was?

It was a joke.

Kobbe Koffi from Togoland!

That's not a joke?

And if you count up the total loss in dollars and cents—if you take into account just the sport coat and the necktie, on the one hand, for instance, and then, on the other, the costs for the emergency room at Mount Sinai and for the overnight truck to get the stuff up to Henry, if you just take those for starters, those specific expenditures for starters—then you will see that in and of itself it was not a cheap joke, either.

Not that Florence and I are exactly starving, mind you—but neither do we have money as such to burn.

I mean, it is not as if we lived in Woodmere, for instance, is it?

Agreed, agreed, anyone can talk to you like a child some of the time—but make no mistake of it, there are times when one must talk to you as a grown-up would, as would a grown-up like anyone else.

I am not a child!

This is the Upper East Side!

She always had the smell of lilac on her. You didn't even have to get up that close enough to her to smell it on her, to smell the lilac which was on the hankie which was on her, which was the hankie which she pinned every day to her bodice, every day a fresh hankie with fresh drops of something with lilac in it.

I tell you, I have been turned the wrong way ever since Kobbe Koffi.

What happened to me?

Something happened to me.

My son is coming home very soon now.

She said it was the fragrance of lilac.

She said fragrance and lilac and bodice.

Here are some of the words she said—she said drops and dewdrops and mist—she said ribbony and whispery and cottony.

She said, "Boys and girls, can you say gossamer?"

You want to hear the words I heard?

I heard quilted and cuticle and petal and sleeve and opal and hosiery and unguent.

I once heard Miss Donnelly say contour

It is very complicated. The idea of this is very complicated. I mean the words and the rhyming—I mean thinking that you were rhyming.

Listen—he fell over.

I think his feet were still in the sandbox.

I think that he still had the rake and that his feet were all of the way inside of the sandbox.

That he had sandals on.

That he had overalls on.

Four white buttons—two front, two back.

Big white ones.

The hoe, I had the hoe. It was the hoe which I had just hit him with. Whereas Andy Lieblich, he had the shovel.

Andy Lieblich always had the shovel.

And a sunsuit on.

His sunsuit on.

The little roof, the little fringed awning, it was up over it—it was flat out up over the sandbox to keep the sun out.

It was broiling.

She said it was broiling.

It was August.

Unless it wasn't fringed, unless the fact is that it actually wasn't.

The trick which I had, the secret which I had, the secret which was just between me and the sandbox, was to dig down in the corner where the sun hadn't gotten because down there the sand was gluey, not just only because it was almost actually like wet actually, but because even in other ways you could almost say that it was more or less different.

You could say that it had more body to it.

For one thing, you could say that it almost felt gluey even.

I'll tell you something else.

This will show you, this will show you—when I tell you how much I used to put all of my heart into it when I was in Andy Lieblich's sandbox playing Farmer with Andy Lieblich, this will really show you how much I really meant it—namely, the fact that you could look at it and think that there was a bug in it of some kind, that there was some kind of bug down there in the sand which was down there, a little round crablike type of sand bug which could roll itself up to look like a pellet of sand when it wanted to, when it had to hide from you before it got set up in the best position to bite you.

You must know what I mean.

Don't you remember when you were six?

I remember.

Like a little ball of it which moved like there was something inside of it which was keeping it going.

Little mind, little feet, little pincers.

Oh, I don't believe that you don't remember what I mean—or how you just had to pick it up and squeeze.

How you, how you yourself, just couldn't not squeeze.

But there was never anything but just more sand in it. There was never any bug in it. Except it didn't matter the next time, did it? I mean, when you saw another little ball of it that looked like it was going all along all by itself—it was always the terror, wasn't it? And then the murder over and over?

With nothing ever dead.

All you ever killed was little clumps of sand.

No goo ever oozed out, no shell ever cracked, nothing squashed was ever there in your hand—all that was ever in it was just more sand.

You remember.

It just took me to show you that you could never forget.

It was languid sand. It was languorous sand.

It took courage to dig down for it. No other boy would do that. I was the only boy who would do that. Andy Lieblich was too delicate to do that.

Just like it took it to feel around for the soap. Or stand and watch for it for when the frankfurters split. Or to keep looking at the colored man when the maid saw me look.

I always knew that she was watching me look.

What was she thinking when I was killing him?

Or maybe people do not have to be thinking anything.

The older I get, the more times there are when I am not thinking anything, or even paying any attention to what I hear myself saying.

It's going to be very hard to tell you about the rhymes. You are going to have to think back with all of your mind to remember what I am going to tell you about the rhymes, or what I think I am going to try to. Because as much as there is any reason for why I killed Steven Adinoff in the year of 1940 and in the town of Woodmere, I think that I have to say that the rhymes probably come as close to it as any—or actually I suppose that I know that they do, that it is the rhymes which comes closest to the reason why I did it, even though, even in that sense, there still wasn't really any real reason. But I don't know how you would go about the whole thing of talking about the rhymes, or if whether there is even a way to.

For one thing—just to begin with, I don't think I mean rhymes in the sense that we in general mean them.

I mean like with like.

I think I mean like with like.

I don't know what I mean.

Take the names Henry and Florence—Florence and Henry—because to me those are rhymes, or almost like rhymes, whereas to somebody else, I don't know what they are to somebody else—all I can do is tell you about my own rhymes.

Or guess at what they were when I killed Steven Adinoff.

Lieblich and Adinoff—Adinoff and Lieblich—do you hear it, do you hear it?

Or this one, this one—Lackawanna 4-1810.

It's not going to be possible.

I am already mixed up.

I think I thought I knew something, but I probably really didn't.

You could wash off the regular sand, but the sand which came from deep down, that was the sand which stayed stuck on sometimes, sometimes it stayed stuck onto your fingers or stuck in up under your fingernails, and even later on, even when you were all washed off, you could sometimes still feel it reminding you that it was still there, actually feel even just one single solitary grain of it pushing up.

No matter how many times I did it, I was still a little surprised all the time. I mean, it was hard to believe it, how it would just go like that, how it would just seem to just go along all by itself like that if there wasn't going to be anything in it but just more sand inside.

I want you to realize something—namely, that he had the shovel to dig down with if he wanted to, whereas I had to use my hand because the hoe was too slow.

I was the colored man when I did it.

I was a lady-in-waiting when I did it.

I was the boy who was ready for the Christians.

I was the boy who liked the smell.

But who were they when I was doing it—who was she in her chair with those things going up and down her wristwatch—and him, who was Andy Lieblich?

Let me tell you this—my Henry is not delicate. Talk about a camper, my Henry is a camper—this Henry of mine is a camper through and through.

Pay attention to me—we live in a world where there are words like torque in it.

Listen to these—torque and carborundum and drogue and dredge.

Do you hear what I am saying to you?

There is everything!

Just think of it of this way—there is nothing that isn't.

And don't think that doesn't go for places, too.

What I actually have in mind, I think, is here and there, here being Ninety-first just off Fifth, there being Eighty-third and Fifth, a distance from one to the other of a little over eight blocks.

My opinion was we could have walked it, and should have walked it, whereas Florence's was taxi, taxi.

Florence's opinion is always taxi, taxi.

What I am getting at, what I am preparing to talk about, is the morning of—namely, how I got my head smashed and my fingers mashed, or what I should probably say instead, what would probably be a more honest way of stating the whole thing instead, scraped and pinched—how I got my head scraped and two fingers pinched.

As I've said, like I've said—you choose, I'm getting tired of choosing for you—the whole thing came to three Band-Aids, it's a three-Band-Aid story—not that that's got anything even close to do with what I think the point of it is, which is that—here goes—the camp gives you these instructions—namely, that if your son is not flying up—the cost of an airline ticket is preposterous, totally preposterous—or not driving up—we don't keep a car, we don't have a car, because of the lunatic costs of what they get for garaging one as such here in Manhattan—then, for a reasonable fee, for a moderately reasonable fee, he can make his way up to camp on a bus the camp charters for the purpose if he will only present himself—on time, on time—in front of the Metropolitan Museum of Art (roughly Eighty-third Street and Fifth Avenue) at eight-thirty, or nine o'clock, I frankly forget which, with his footlocker and his duffel bag in his personal possession at the time.

Now there you have it.

I am no fool, I tell you.

That was the situation.

I forget which day—I mentioned it a little bit earlier—late June, the end of June, the date is not important—it's a weekday, it's a weekday—if anything is important, then it's that it was a weekday that's important and that I went ahead and laid out for a new sport coat and a new necktie by way of making myself presentable, by way of at least doing my best, for Henry's sake, to not make a less than good impression on the other parents, on the other campers, on any camp counselors that might turn out to be riding along and so on and so forth.

What I am saying is that between us, even with the footlocker and with the duffel bag, it wouldn't have been any big deal for us to have walked it, with Henry and me handling the actual manpower and with Florence just walking with us. But I will admit that it was a slightly insane morning to begin with. For one thing, the two of us, Florence and I, we'd been up to all hours packing up the last of Henry's things and getting the rest of his labels sewn on everything they weren't sewn on yet, and all of his other stuff marked with his name and meanwhile knocking together a list of every single solitary item the boy is taking up—and then there was that whole thing of what I happened to catch sight of on television, so who could sleep after that?

No, I was not myself in the morning.

Yes, I was more than normally distracted in the morning.

But make no mistake of it—I still insist, however, that there was totally no need for a taxi—on that point I don't see any reasonable argument to the contrary.

There is no legitimate argument to the contrary.

No one is saying that it is a question of money.

It was not a question of money.

However, it definitely is a question of money now—when you stop to consider what this little episode has cost me—yes, yes, yes, yes, it certainly, from every aspect, is a definite question of money now, plus the fact that I have been able to think of hardly nothing other since—namely, this totally clownish little episode, the famous Three-Band-Aid Episode, it almost looks to me like it has turned me looking rearward for keeps.

I mean, I don't really see any more future for me, whereas I tell you, I tell you, that's unacceptable, that's unacceptable—for one thing, Henry's expected home before you know it—and for another, I can't do this to Florence.

She is not the one who killed anybody!

My wife and son, my wife and child, you think they even know where Woodmere is?

His feet, he had sandals on—I saw sandals on—whereas I do not see my own feet as to speak about shoes and socks, as to be certain about shoes and socks.

I see a lime-green sport coat—and a Squadron A necktie—both from Dunhill's, and neither one of them cheap!

Imagine it, imagine it—a telephone number you haven't heard, you hadn't heard, in how many years?

I want you to think of something.

What if Henry hadn't made the bus?

I'm the one who could touch that sand, hear that shoe, look at what that hoe did.

Look while it was doing it.

Kids are stronger today. No question about it, kids are much stronger today. It doesn't matter what social rank they come from, what kind of background they come from, they are all much stronger these days.

They are tremendously stronger these days.

For instance, I actually couldn't turn the handle of the meat grinder or of the clothes wringer for my mother—in all honesty and sincerity, I couldn't, I actually couldn't.

I'm going to tell you something—which is that I was proud of the fact that we had a clothes wringer, but I wish that we had had it standing somewhere else and not always out in the garage with the door wide open for the whole world to see it.

And the clothesline always up between the poles, they didn't have to have that up all of the time. It wasn't always sunny enough to have that up all of the time. And yet I always think of summer, of summer, and never not of a day when the colored man couldn't have come for the Buick because it was too rainy or blowy or snowy.

I wish I was six years old.

She said we had to keep things where they were because it was the landlord who made us.

I used to have meatloaf from the meat she ground up, or a hamburger fried in the frypan. I never had things broiled. She said she didn't even know what a meat pattie was, that she had never even heard of anything which was called anything like it. She said couldn't I tell her what I meant. She said for me to just tell her what it was. She said for me to just describe it.

I never told her the names of the things which the colored man said.

But look at Henry, look at Henry!

I remember a sound like the sound that you would say sogginess would have if sogginess were something which could have its own special sound. I remember that—and even the sound of slowing down, of a kind of slowing down, and of the tingling I told you about, the buzziness up deep inside of my backside—and rhymes—rhymes and rhymes and rhymes in my head.

It was a question of obeying the rule.

It was a question of obeying the biggest one of her rules.

Plain and simple, pure and simple, it was all a question of the rules—and I did not make the rules, I did not make the rules.

Even now, even now, do I make the rules even now?

If I made the rules, we would have walked.

Plain and simple, pure and simple.

Walked!

It was just a toy. They were just toys.

I think they used to call them peewee-size.

Or just peewee.

A peewee hoe, a peewee rake.

There was a baseball player named that—because he was small, I suppose. Not that I knew about him then. I did not know anything about baseball. I did not care anything about baseball. How was I supposed to know anything about Johnny Mize? I didn't care anything about Johnny Mize. I didn't care anything about any of them—Johnny Mize, Peewee Reese—whatever all of their names were. I never cared anything about any of them, not even to this day. I only know about Johnny Mize because of Steven Adinoff—and Peewee Reese, him I don't even know how I know about.

Let them ask Henry.

Ask Henry.

Henry knows baseball inside out.

All of the sports, sports in general—not just the sport of baseball in particular.

Andy Lieblich had a peewee lawnmower to make believe he was mowing his lawn with. Iris Lieblich had peewee things like that, too. Maybe everybody did—I don't know.

Maybe the reason we didn't have a lawn was because of the coal itself—or was because of the Blue Coal truck having to always drive up so close to get the chute to reach over to the cellar window.

I would like to be six years old and have her looking down at me with me looking up at her and seeing her see my place.

Here's one of the things the nanny used to say—she said that if you wanted to keep having the best lawn on the block, then you couldn't have little boys ever getting sand in it.

She said nothing came for free, that you got what you paid for, that if you wanted to have nice things, then you had to pay good money for them—she said that contrary to popular opinion, that the Lieblichs were not made of money, that they did not just go pick money off of trees, that they did not coin money or have money to burn or money burning a hole in their pocket or money to throw away or to put a match to or to just pour down the drain, that they didn't mint money and weren't rolling in money, that they weren't rich people from being chiselers or from cutting corners or from squeezing every last nickel and every red cent.

She said the lawn was my responsibility even if it wasn't mine.

She said that I had responsibilities.

This is what she said—"A place for everything, and everything in its place."

This is what she said—"Let it never be said, and said to your shame, that all was beauty here before you came."

There is something which I have been saving up to tell you, something which I have just gotten ready to tell you—which is that I used to sometimes just go take off my shoes and my socks and go walking on it—just go walking on it over near where it was close to my own property—just go ahead and walk on it on my bare feet and think to myself that it felt like the way it would be feeling to a lady-in-waiting who was walking on her own property in a storybook place.

You haven't even turned the corner yet, they haven't even driven you all of two feet yet, and right off the bat the tariff's already a dollar ten—it's a dollar ten for just turning the meter on—and then guess what you've got to pay out through the nose for each ninth of a mile after that.

Ten cents.

That's what they get for a measly ninth of a mile, but don't waste your breath being amazed by it.

It isn't the money, it isn't the money—it's just this whole thing of needless spending, of totally wasteful spending—when what would it have been to just go ahead and pick the stuff up and walk it a handful of blocks?

Plus which, wouldn't Henry himself have gotten a big extra kick out of it? I mean, the chance to show off his muscles?

He lifts weights, you know.

His share of the footlocker, his end of it, and even all of the duffel bag, it wouldn't have been any big thing for him.

She used to say share and share alike.

It's nice.

Listen.

156

Share and share alike.

I wonder if it's one they still say, that's still said.

The DeSoto—do they still make a DeSoto?

They make Buicks.

Who can tell me about my shoes and socks? In all the world, in all of the whole wide world, there is no one I can go ask about my shoes and socks. Or probably even just about Woodmere.

I did not expect someone to fall over. I did not expect anyone to fall down. I was probably more amazed than he was that a little peewee-size hoe could do a thing like that, make someone fall over just like that.

Couldn't the rake have done the same thing?

It could all be a question of that—of who lies down first, or just of who wants to lie down more.

What if I stopped using mineral oil?

Then what?

In both cases, in both instances, in the case of the footlocker and the lid of the trunk, and in the case of the duffel bag and the back door, nothing would have happened if I hadn't reached back, or reached in, or whatever.

And each time for what, for what?

The thing about me is that I believe in God—and believe that other people do.

No one rushed to help me, by the way. No one

even inquired. And make no mistake of it, I didn't look like just some maniac on the street—I was more than presentable—that jacket, that tie?

They all just gaped—or looked away.

No, no one looked away.

I was right the first time—everyone gaped, everyone looked. If anyone turned, it was to look, not to look away.

They saw me.

Good.

Sir saw me, too—and I saw Sir.

I'm going to tell you what I know—we are all on our backs, waiting for them to look.

Just like dogs.

Or me.

Or like Steven Adinoff was.

We had to walk everywhere unless we got lifts. He had to walk everywhere unless he got lifts. I sometimes used to hear her tell him to hurry up and get out there so that the Lieblichs would see him and give him a lift. But I never went to look to see if they did.

I'll tell you something I used to think—I used to think why didn't he wear corduroys like I did?

It was the most Christian smell of all.

The smell of lilac was the most Christian one of all.

It was just blocks to the Woodmere Academy, but

158

it was forever to P.S. #5. However, after I killed Steven Adinoff, my school was P.S. #3, which wasn't anywhere close to being anywhere near as long of a walk. On the other hand, I don't remember a thing about any of it— the walk, the teacher, the school. I just remember that it was P.S. #3 and the DeSoto on the new block.

You can't beat Vernax for shoes. They make it for furniture, but I say that you cannot beat it for shoes.

It's almost a hobby of mine, the polishing of shoes.

It's me that does Henry's and Florence's.

I'll squat there with my shoebrush and my Vernax. I'll go, "Rub a dub dub, three men in a tub." I could kill a Saturday afternoon just doing them, just polishing theirs and mine.

That's the only thing which wasn't a loss, which was maybe even a gain in a way—namely, the fact that they're probably even in what you could say is better shape now than they were in the first place—the leather, after I got the blood off of them, or at least the Vernax on over it.

We had the sound, we had the volume all the way down. For one thing, let's not forget that Henry was sleeping. Besides which, it was what? Two, almost two? Maybe even later. You can't go around with the television blasting away at that hour in a building of this quality.

Here's something I know.

The way which I saw that was the way which she saw us.

Make no mistake of it, it's totally normal.

You just like go to sleep looking.

I tell you, I tell you, nothing could be more normal—everybody going to sleep, everybody went to sleep, even Steven Adinoff.

It's like rub a dub dub, three men in a tub.

It's like everything they say.

It's like "Phil! Phil! Is that you? Is that you?"

Or Lackawanna 4-1810.

I don't know.

Kale.

Okra.

Collards.

Turnip greens.

Mustard greens.

Chard.

Chicory.

Squash.

Those were the ones. Those were the eight.

Here's another point—the fact that we always could have put the footlocker down and rested—that there's no law that says we would have had to walk it the whole way there without resting.

Not that I think, I don't actually think that it would have been necessary for Henry to rest.

Actually, there's nothing stopping me from testing it, is there? I mean, the whole thing could be put to a test, couldn't it? But wouldn't that seem petty and small-minded?

In all fairness, I don't think Florence would see it just as me being petty and small-minded if I suggested, if when the time comes, if when we go to pick Henry up, if I just more or less urge the point that we go ahead and try it from Eighty-third to Ninety-first.

All it takes is for him to get home.

Even stronger from a summer of growth.

You had to see it for yourself. How weak they looked, for one thing—how weak they looked when they were killing each other, and the third man—if there really was one, if there really was another man, an extra one, a third man—how weak that one, if there actually was that extra one, how weak he looked, too.

Or maybe they were just all sleepy—that and plus the fact that they felt like being girls.

Big men, I suppose.

Convicts, I suppose—convicts and guards, I suppose—or maybe just convicts. But who knows, who knows, maybe just guards. It probably didn't matter which ones you were.

It didn't matter to Steven Adinoff which one he was.

You had to choose. When it came to the sandbox, the whole thing of it was that you had to make up your mind and choose, even though it was the nanny who was the one who was really doing it, even though you knew that it really was her, you still had to act like you were making up your mind about it and making a choice—because that was her rule—namely, that you choose.

I liked Farmer best.

I didn't like the hoe best.

I liked the hoe second best.

Nobody ever got the rake until Steven Adinoff came along—nobody ever had to have it until Steven Adinoff had to have it—and the reason he had to have it was because this time there were three boys and there wasn't anything else.

She went to her chair and sat down on the slats.

He came around and hooked it up.

It made a sound like something frying far away—and the sound of them, they were just the sound of rubberbands snapping the way they do when they turn over on themselves.

She used to run the water to try to get me going, but that never worked. Nothing ever worked until the mineral oil worked.

I could sit for hours.

I could go for days.

I used to worry when she ran the water that she might have put it on hot without thinking and that the landlord would come over and catch her.

When his mother came, that's where I was.

I was on the toilet.

Whereas with Henry, God bless him, nothing could be more natural—no fuss, no bother—the boy just goes in there and sits himself down and does his business.

I have been waiting for God to reach down and make me stop saying these things. But did God even reach down when it was the sandbox?

I just thought of something.

Maybe it will be a curse on you for just hearing all of this.

Tell the truth, tell the truth, didn't you just get just a little bit scared?

God didn't lift a finger. She didn't, either. And you know why?

Because no one wanted them to.

Not even he himself.

How can you say you don't hear it when a head is getting chopped open?

She saw. She heard. We all did.

I also got him in the face.

She said she wouldn't go down the second time unless it was okay if he came along, too.

I tell you, it wasn't that I myself wanted to look at hers.

His thing came out. She got his thing to come out—or she got me to. I couldn't believe it, I couldn't believe it—I didn't know that it was just his place—what I thought was this—I thought we had wounded him.

When I came in from killing him, she was coming down the stairs—she was on the stairs.

Then we were all three of us just lying back like that, our three different kinds of places showing.

Someone would say, "Reggie, darling, the child needs air."

She went back up and then came back down with the washcloth.

We didn't lie back all of the way. The way you would do it was to lie back but still lean up just enough so that you could still see them looking back down at you while you were showing your place.

I am going to tell you the most amazing thing I know.

That's even what he did.

What Sir did.

A dog!

Listen to me—I know something—I know what I saw in the sandbox, I know what I saw on the roof.

She went back up and then came back down with it. The idea of it was, I could tell that the idea of it was for her to have something which she could use to wash the blood off, something to wash off the blood from where he got me with the rake.

But then she just sat down on the floor.

But then she didn't do anything with it, but then she just sat down with it in her lap—and I saw it that it was making a mess there, that it was making a big mess in her lap because when she went back up to get it, when she had gone back up to get it, she had gotten it so soppy-wet.

Where it was just inside the front door, the first thing was linoleum, the floor there was linoleum, we had linoleum there, there just in front of the front door, so that's what you first heard it on, you heard it first on linoleum whenever he first came home, and then you heard it on wood as he started up the stairs.

I want you to know this—there wasn't anything else to get the Blue Coal dust off of his place with.

There wasn't any screaming. From start to finish, no one screamed. He didn't scream and the nanny didn't scream and Andy Lieblich definitely didn't, either. There wasn't even any talking even, except for when he said "Nyou nyon't nyave nyoo nyill nyee," and "Nyou nyidn't nyave nyoo nyill nyee," and those other things about the card with the baseball player on it.

When all is said and done, neither did my mother—she just sat down on the floor with the washcloth in her lap. She just stayed like that. She just stayed there like that with the washcloth in her lap. I don't know if she knew that he was home until she heard him yell "Reg!" But I did.

I always heard him.

I always heard everything.

I wasn't thinking much. I was probably still making up rhymes instead of starting to think again much. But I know what one of the things which I was thinking was—namely, were we going to have to buy the Lieblichs new sand for the sand which I was getting messed up?

Plus a hoe.

The rake, the rake, I didn't even feel it where it had gotten stuck in me and wasn't going to come loose until he had gotten going yanking up on it at the same time as when I was yanking downward on it so that both together we could see if we could get it to work itself the rest of the way out.

The other thing was, I didn't want to try to take the washcloth out of her lap.

It's amazing, it's amazing, what someone almost dead will do.

He was almost dead when he did that, got me with the rake and then helped me get it back out.

His face made a different sound than his head did.

Then when there was just the handle of the hoe left, then it was all different—just from the standpoint of sound even.

You have to imagine dents—like a trench—in his hair, in his head. Whereas with his face, it was more like a peach pit with some of the peach still left on it.

I say his face, but what I really mean, the part which I am actually talking about, it wasn't his whole face, of course—what I mean is his cheek when I say his face, the cheek up on one side up high on it just under the eye on that side.

I never got anywhere near the harelip itself.

You know how part of the peach pit will look dry? You have seen that, haven't you? It is a little bit surprising, the dryness which is in the look of it. But in all reality, it is just a question of the look that it has to it. Because if you touched it, it would be wet, wouldn't it?

Imagine a boy who grows up liking the word chamois—imagine a boy like that, imagine him in comparison with one who grows up liking the word carborundum—do you think they would have the same religions?

Or here's an even better question—do you think a person can grow up liking no words at all?

Automatically?
Theoretically?

Maybe some of the times when I wasn't allowed to come over, maybe some of the times when I didn't have her permission to come over, maybe times when she said to me that Andy Lieblich had to play the field, maybe those were times when it was Steven Adinoff who was actually there in my place—maybe he was the boy who was always there when I couldn't be, when she wouldn't let me be, when she would say to me things like Rome wasn't built in a day, tomorrow is another day, every dog will have his day, let the lesson be sufficient unto the day thereof.

She used to say to me that milk without the chill off was poison.

I still don't know what a shirred egg is. Or a coddled one.

I never thought of this before, but maybe they're eggs made in some kind of way where you couldn't even eat it unless you had an egg cup to hold them in.

I actually thought she was going to nyalk nyike nyis too. When my mother was calling me to get off and come down and just let her look at me and talk to me, I thought she was going to nyalk nyust nyike nyee nyid until I killed him.

It was meant to be a gift to me, that thing about her brassiere.

You know these things when you are six. You make no mistakes about things like this when you are six. She wished she could have had me instead. That way she wouldn't have had to have been a mother who was glad to have a boy who was dead. How would you like to be a mother who had to kiss her boy on a lip like that? There's no choice, there's no choice. You think he wouldn't feel it if you kissed him even just a little bit to the side of it? I tell you, you'd have to kiss him good-night right on it—and even then you wouldn't fool him one bit, not one single bit—because just imagine how he could feel everything with it, how he would have learned to detect everything with it, how he would have learned to test out the world with it, how he would have learned to divine your whole heart with it—plus every smidgen of what went into, or did not go into, the quality, the character, the deep structure of your kiss.

Listen to me—the world isn't people and the situations which they are in, it's situations and the people which are in them!

My God, my God, you couldn't even miss it by accident, suppose you just missed it by accident. But you think he'd hate you any less for always kissing him right on it dead center?

I tell you, it's not even funny how much that woman owed me for, how much Steven Adinoff's mother owed me for. But not that she didn't make an effort to pay it.

You know what?

Money doesn't measure just money—money measures everything. You can't name something which money doesn't measure—unless you just don't know what money is, or are afraid to.

What is a ninth of a mile?

Measured in city blocks, in relation to city blocks, I would really like for someone to come along and tell me.

Some families don't have kissing on the lips. Some families have totally, but totally different arrangements. Some families, even the whole question of kissing itself doesn't even come up as a thing to begin with, whereas you could never say that about money, could you?

How it went, how exactly it went in terms of every last detail of it, in relation to all of the things in particular of it, that I can't tell you, that I can't tell you—but what I can tell you is how it went in general, in the sense of right in the middle of everything, in the sense of her stopping things right in the middle of everything and saying this thing about either I myself had to leave the room for a minute and then could come right back or that she had to and that she would be right back, and then one or the other of us going from the kitchen to the living room for a minute or from the living room to the kitchen for a minute and then coming right back to whichever room which it was that she had been taking a look at me in in the first place, and then hearing it, hearing it, hearing her say it and knowing that she was saying it strictly for my benefit, that she was saying it to my mother loud enough for me to hear it on purpose, on purpose—namely, "It was binding me."

It.

I knew what it meant.

She knew that I would know what it meant, that I would know what she meant by it.

But then she put her hands up under underneath the bottoms of them and moved them around a little bit to make sure.

It made me think of a place for everything and everything in its place.

It made me think of muslin, of russet, of homespun.

You know what I used to sometimes do? I'd think to myself, I'd sometimes think to myself that Mr. and Mrs. Lieblich were going to come outside and see me standing watching the colored man while he was washing or waxing the Buick, I'd stand there thinking to myself that any instant Mr. and Mrs. Lieblich were going to suddenly come out of their house and see me standing there and then say to themselves how nice I looked and that there was a big mistake which had been made way back along the line somewhere and that I myself was actually their real boy and that Andy Lieblich wasn't.

I tell you, I tell you, there were times when I could just feel myself standing naked in gossamer.

I was always waiting—for them or for somebody. I was always the one who was waiting. Even when I was sitting on the toilet, who ever waited as much as I did?

I wonder if he's already strong enough to kill me. I think in theory that he is already strong enough to kill me.

I want to know something.

I want to know how come I always feel like I am waiting, as if they've singled me out to be the one who is waiting.

I never saw them. I never actually saw them that I actually know of. I just saw the Buick come out of the garage or go into the garage—I just saw the Buick when it was coming with them or going with them.

No one ever had to tell me that it was better than a DeSoto. But I think that there was someone who did, anyway.

It's really amazing to you when a person falls down from something which you yourself have just done to them, when they just stop doing what they were doing and fall right down right in front of you.

And then lie there, looking up at you, waiting.

Like I did, like she did, like even like Sir did.

I think the best description of his lip was to go do what she made me do and see it when it comes out.

Does it sting for it to be out in the air like that? Is that how it was when the shoe was off of it, like the air itself could make it feel too chilly for it, or that just the dust in the air was going to get all over it and stick to it and not come off of it without it really hurting you?

Nobody was saying they could still smell it the next day, but I could still do it. Even in school, I could. Even with the lilac, I could. And the hoses, I could see those.

I thought that we had wounded him, that the thing that came out of him was what you saw when you had wounded him, and that that's how we'd be caught when she took him by the collar and went home with him—that when she went home with him, they would go ahead and take a look at him and then make her tell them where she was with him that he got that way like that and who did it to him, was it me who wounded him? Whereas with Steven Adinoff, no one had to ask.

I couldn't make up my mind which smell I liked better, that one or the one of lilac. Plus the ones of cocoa butter and of citronella.

I wonder which one was Henry's favorite when he himself was of an age like that. But you'd never know from asking. A child would never tell.

You were six.

So don't you have to know?

Don't you remember how you always had such high hopes whenever you got your things on and went out?

That's all I always did.

I always had such high hopes.

I just went out.

But all day long there was no one to play with, and the colored man didn't come, and the Blue Coal truck wasn't going to come, and there wasn't going to be any school to go to, either—what about my mother, was she having someone over, was there going to be anyone anywhere for me to look at and have for company?

It was August.

I didn't even have my corduroys on.

It was strictly for my benefit, strictly for my benefit.

She knew that I would know she meant brassiere.

THE ROOF

There wasn't anyone.

There wasn't anything.

There was just the day which was so hot and sitting on the curb and thinking to myself. I don't know, I can't say, I can't actually remember, but chances are, it stands to reason, it's probably in all truth a fact that I was already making up rhymes even at that point right then and there while I was sitting on the curb. I mean, it's what you did to keep yourself company—just started with this and then went to that and then kept on going and going—saying to yourself, let's say saying to yourself "It's hot," "It's lot," "It's not," "It's top," "It's mop," "It's nop," "Tip top," "Sip sop," "Hip hop," and so on and so forth—on and on and on—more and more getting the idea that if you just keep it up and don't get tired, then you're going to be the first person in the world to rhyme every word there is—or have to stop to vomit from trying.

You know.

Everybody knows.

There isn't anybody who doesn't do it.

Or who didn't.

It's the closest you ever get to feel that you yourself are God—or that if there wasn't any God, then that this would be the same thing which was, that it was God which could rhyme all of the words, or at least which did it once.

But there is a God, so you give up.

It's too complicated.

However, you don't need me to tell you what I mean. You were six. We were all the same.

So it was hot and it was Woodmere and this was August in the year of 1940 and there wasn't anyone and there wasn't anything, and in my head, all to myself, I was probably saying rhymes and sitting in front of my property on the curb.

And what was next was this.

My mother called out of the window for me to come in and get my lunch, that there was a sandwich of meatloaf for me to get in the kitchen and a bottle of chocolate drink for me in the icebox and then to go back outside and have it so that the house would stay clean because maybe the landlord was coming over.

I am trying to think and see the shoes and socks I had on, but I cannot see them.

The next thing was the Buick coming!

The next thing was looking up and seeing the Buick coming!

The next thing was not knowing what to do next because I saw the Buick coming!

It came down past the Woodmere Academy and then came into the block and then turned and went up along their driveway and then through their garage door and into that darkness.

That darkness, that particular darkness which you could see when you looked in through their garage door, it always looked to me like the special darkness of rich people to me, like nice darkness, velvety darkness, with like a kind of special nice wateriness to it that made it better than what other people had.

The nanny came out into the driveway.

But there weren't any children who did.

I didn't see Andy Lieblich or Iris Lieblich or Mr. or Mrs. Lieblich. I didn't see anybody but the nanny there. It was just her with her uniform and her arms and her wristwatch and her rubberbands.

She said, "Look who's here." She said, "Is it hot enough for you?" She said, "You could fry an egg on the sidewalk." She said, "That's how hot it is, you could fry an egg on the sidewalk." She said, "What are you eating there, bologna and soda?" She said, "Isn't your mother feeding you light?" She said, "Heat like this, you have to eat light." She said, "Go tell your mother to feed you light." She said, "Lettuce and leafy vegetables." She said, "What is your mother feeding you?" She said, "You shouldn't eat bologna and soda." She said, "That's poison in any weather." She said, "Tell your mother I said so." She said, "Go tell her." She said, "Somebody should tell the woman not to put anything too heavy on your stomach." She said, "Fruits, fresh fruits." She said, "Go tell her to give you an apple at least." She said, "Throw it away." She said, "Take my advice and throw the rest of it away." She said, "In heat like this, you're killing yourself. Be smart," she said. "Get rid of it, whatever it is."

I said, "Did Andy just come home?" I said, "Did Iris?" I said, "Who was in the Buick with you—was Andy, was Andy?"

180

She said, "Andy, Andy, Andy." She said, "It's always Andy, Andy, Andy." She said, "Morning, noon, and night, what is it but Andy, Andy, Andy!"

I said, "Is Andy there? Is he inside?"

She said, "You just finish your lunch like a good little fellow and we will see what we will see." She said, "You get it all down and then go have your nap and then we will see what we will see when you're all rested and fresh and not overheated." She said, "You go tell your mother to fix you a nice cool bath and then put you down for a nice refreshing nap and then we will see what we will see." She said, "After Andrew has had his lunch, then we will see what we will see." She said, "Didn't anybody ever tell you it's not good for you to be out in the middle of the day when it's a day like this?" She said, "Doesn't your mother ever tell you anything?"

I didn't have to listen to her. I could just listen to the rubberbands.

I said, "Is Iris inside?" I said, "Can Iris come out and play?"

But the nanny just turned around and went back inside of the garage. Then there was a long time when I just sat on the curb again. Then the same thing happens again, looking up again and seeing something, seeing the colored man rolling the Buick out, this time seeing the colored man rolling out the Buick, seeing the colored man there at the Lieblichs' all of a sudden right out of the blue.

I said, "I didn't see you." I said, "Did you just come over?"

He kept rolling the Buick out, he kept rolling out the Buick.

I said, "I didn't see you." I said, "Did you just come over?"

He went and got things from the step in front of the screen door and from the hooks and from the shelves. He went and got everything—he got some rags and the sponge and the whiskbroom and the dust pan and the chamois cloth and the scrub brush and the Old Dutch and then set them all out and then went back in and changed shirts.

Then she came out again and said to me, "What did I say to you? Didn't I tell you to go home and take a nap?"

I said, "Can Andy come out and play?"

She said, "You are getting yourself overexcited and overheated." She said, "You are going to have to learn how to cooperate with others." She said, "There is a time and a place for everything." She said, "Go home and take a nap." She said, "Tell your mother I said that you look sallow from the heat." She said, "All in due course." She said, "We shall see what we shall see." She said, "Slow and steady wins the race." She said, "What did you do with that poison you were eating?" She said, "Did you eat that poison?" She said, "Get away from here and let him work."

Then there was another long time again with me back sitting on the curb. Maybe I was saying to myself, maybe I was thinking to myself, "It's poison," "It's moison," "It's soison."

I don't know.

Something like that.

Something probably like that.

I knew, I always knew—you could always tell it when what she was actually doing was just trying to make you wait. In all honesty and sincerity, you always knew when you could count on it for her to finally come back out.

This time this is what she said—she said, "Do you still want to play?"

She said, "Go tell your mother if you still want to play."

She said, "Go home and wash your hands and tell your mother I said it's okay for her to send you over if you still want to play."

I was so excited.

I was always so excited.

I didn't know that this was going to be the day

when I was going to kill someone. All I could think of was of the sandbox, was of being in the sandbox, of getting her permission to be in it and play.

Then there was another long time again of me waiting at their back door and then of her coming out and saying, "Patience is a virtue. Rome wasn't built in a day. Go away for a while and then come back later, Andrew and Iris and their guest are just starting on their salads now, share and share alike, a watched pot never boils, there's all the time in the world," and then of her going back inside and of me just staying there.

I wonder if the glue smell was from what they made the shoe of, or from what they had to put all the leather together with. I wonder if it really was a pink color and wet-looking, or if that was just the crazy thing I thought because of the other things I saw. I wonder why he didn't say "Reg! Reg!" the way she herself said "Phil! Phil!" I wonder how come they didn't know that it would have been nicer for me to have that to listen to.

I tried to keep from looking at the sandbox.

I tried to keep from thinking about the colored man.

Maybe I was thinking about the watched pot and the frankfurters, about me having to be the one who had to watch them until you could see the splits open up in them both.

Then she was at the screen door again. She said,

"All's well that ends well," and pushed it open and came out, and right behind her there he was, there he was, and I wanted to jump up and down and up and down and go hug him and take him by the hand, take him by the hand and hold his hand and say "Andy! Andy!"

Which is when another boy came out and the nanny said to me, "Say hello to Steven Adinoff. This is Andrew's guest, Steven Adinoff. He has a deformity, but he is not going to let you make him ashamed of it. He has a harelip, but don't you dare try to make him ashamed of it. A harelip is the last thing in the world that anyone has to stand around and be ashamed of. If I had a harelip, do you think that I would be ashamed of it for even one instant? A harelip is nothing to be ashamed of. I promise you, when you have one, no one even notices it, no one even cares."

I felt so wonderful from the feeling which I was having. It was like I was suddenly going from the worst day in the world to the best day in the world. I just couldn't wait for it to really get started. I just couldn't wait for us to get everything else over and done with. It gave me the worst feeling which you could imagine, just me having to stop to realize all of the different things which we were going to have to get out of the way first before we could really get going and get started. It gave me the feeling of someone sitting on me, of someone the size of the colored man just sitting on me and telling me that he wasn't going to get off of me until he got good and ready to. For instance, did I even have her permission yet? I didn't even have her permission yet. And what about the rule about you could never have more than two boys at a time in the sandbox, what about it just in general—and then what about what was going to happen if she said it could only be two boys in particular, then what about which two boys it was going to be, Andy Lieblich and which other one?

Plus picking the game, plus which one was going to be the game—was it going to be Farmer or Gardener or Builder—and the new boy, was he going to get to be the one to choose? Whereas if he did, if he actually did, then was that going to mean that after Andy Lieblich picked the shovel, then the new boy was just going to automatically go next and then get to have the hoe and that I would have to have the rake in and of itself?

I tell you, it was like someone sitting down on my chest. It was like sitting on the toilet and knowing that you are going to have to sit on it forever before you can finally get up.

I just wanted to get things started and get going. It was so hot. It all felt to me like it was so slow—it felt to me like it all was starting to go even slower. I kept waiting for her to get everything taken care of. But she just sat in the slatted chair and kept rolling the rubberbands up and down and saying that she had to think all sorts of different things over, that Rome was not built in a day, that we have to share and share alike, that the last shall be the first and vice versa.

There was the baseball card. He had a baseball card. He kept trying to tell me about it. I could tell that he wanted to be friends with me and that he thought that getting me to look at his baseball card was the best way for him to do it, for him to be friends with me. He kept trying to get me to take the baseball card and look at it. He wouldn't stop trying to get me to take it from him and take a look at it. But I wasn't going to touch anything which he had ever touched. Stop and think a minute—in all frankness, did I know what a harelip was? I didn't know if you could catch it. How could I tell if someone could catch it? If it was catching, then wouldn't you catch it if you touched something which someone who had it touched?

"Nyonny Nyize," he said.

I said, "What?"

"Nyonny Nyize," he said.

I said, "What?"

He said, "Nyonny Nyize." He said, "Nyee nyays nyirst nyase nyor nya Nyaint Nyouis Nyardnyals."

187

I still don't know anything about baseball—and don't want to. When it comes to baseball, I leave it all to Henry and Florence, I leave them all of the honors—those two, they just can't get enough of it—whereas me, the only thing I know less about than I know about baseball is, say, football, for instance—or, in all actuality, any other sport as such—I myself just don't care about sports in general, especially not the kinds of sports which Henry does, which are all of the ones which I happen to think are the ones which are on the expensive side—skiing, for instance—water-skiing in the summertime and regular skiing in the winter.

That's what his camp has a specific emphasis in, they have it in water-skiing—speedboats and water skis and those special life jackets water-skiers wear, they have all of those things up there, the camp is specifically set up for it.

They couldn't be bigger than they are on water-skiing up there.

She said, "It takes all kinds to make a world."

I thought to myself that it might be a game, that it might be a trick, that it might be a secret between all three of them, that the way he was talking might really just be a secret which all three of them, which they were all three of them actually having against me.

I thought to myself that he had been inside, hadn't he? I thought to myself that if he had been inside, then didn't that mean that he was in on it, that now he was in on what a meat pattie was, that now he was in on the secret of that, and of the egg cup and the maid.

I'll tell you one of the things which made me feel the worst I ever felt—namely, it was this—that Andy Lieblich probably knew things about baseball and who Johnny Mize was. One of the things which made me feel the worst I ever felt was having that particular thought.

She said, "All that child is doing is just trying to join in like any normal child."

The colored man came around. I watched him hook the hose up. He let the hose fall down from around his arm and dumped it down on the ground under the faucet and then he hooked it up.

My God, it was all so hot and so slow and so itchy. It wasn't the way the Lieblichs' usually was. She was right—there were too many boys and it was too hot and things were at sixes and sevens.

She said, "Raise your hand if you want to be one of the boys who plays in the sandbox today."

It made a hissy sound. It made a sound like when you hear the frying in a frying pan from far away.

She said, "I am just one woman alone—I can't undo the nature of everything."

189

It was like being upstairs and listening to her down in the kitchen.

I said, "If Andy gets the shovel, can I have the hoe and he has to have the rake?"

It was a sound of sizzling.

I kept on hearing it even though it kept on getting farther and farther away.

She said, "I am just one person alone—I cannot be expected to change the nature of everything."

You have to stop to realize that it could have happened to anybody, the kind of accident which happened to me on June whatever it was, late last June. I mean, it was really just an ordinary thing, a totally ordinary situation and a totally ordinary thing—with the two exceptions of, first, the name of the cab driver and where the cab driver came from, and, second, of the fact that nobody but a total fussbudget would have reached back in the first time and then gone ahead and instantly done the same idiotic thing all over again almost in the very next instant.

But did I have my wits about me? How could I have had my wits about me? There was no way for me to have had my wits about me.

No, I definitely did not have my wits about me, and I think that we can thank the night before for that— that plus the fact that I kept thinking to myself that in

this one specific instance a taxi was needlessly spendthrift and that it might have been nice for Henry to get
a chance to show off in front of the other boys, let them
see what lifting weights had done for him over the winter, let them see him managing to walk his gear over
and so on and so forth—all those things that matter to
teenage boys.

You know what thirteen-year-olds are like. Thirteen-year-olds are like that.

It is really the worst age for comparisons.

Theatrics, hysterics, the whole thing was all just a
question of theatrics and hysterics, and yet at the time, I
tell you, at the time I think I really and truly thought to
myself that it was curtains, that I'd gone ahead and gotten my brains bashed in by some taxi driver just because
I couldn't bear to see a little snippet of something stuck
to the top of a footlocker, some kind of plastic tape or
something—I can't tell you what exactly it was, probably
some kind of friction tape which Henry uses for something and which got stuck there or some masking tape
or Scotch tape from when Florence taped the inventory
up inside the lid of Henry's footlocker.

My God, my God, my knees actually buckled. For
the first time in my life I actually felt what it feels like
to have your knees buckle. Because it's amazing, they
really do, they really buckle—it's actually comic the way
you can feel them buckle like that and then think to

191

yourself, "My God, look at that, my knees are buckling."

Agreed, agreed, I was half out on my feet in the first place.

I'd been up all night.

I'd been up half the night.

I hadn't even gotten a wink of sleep the night before to begin with.

I mean, even if you set aside what I'd seen on television, even if you take what I'd seen and set that aside, just the mere fact of expecting Henry to take off for camp in the morning, even if you just take that fact alone, that probably would have been more than enough to keep me up all night any night, anyway.

The way he got up was like the way they got up on the television.

Or the way at least one of them did. But maybe they both got up again like that—or even the third man, if there really was a third man. He was almost all dead himself, but he got up to walk around and put his hands in his pockets and then get the rake again and then try to get me with it even though he himself was already so far gone that it wasn't even funny anymore, even though he was probably almost already dead by then.

But he put it back down again and then lay back down again.

The blood which I noticed the most was the blood which was on his buttons.

He said, "Nyere's Nyonny Nyize?"

He kept putting his hands in his pockets and feeling all around in them and taking them out and then putting them back in again.

He said, "Nyi nyost Nyonny Nyize."

He kept walking around.

It was unbelievable to me. I really couldn't understand how he could walk around like that anymore, but he kept walking around—in the sandbox, out of the sandbox—he just kept it up and kept putting his hands in his pockets and saying that, saying different things about his baseball card.

I didn't have his baseball card!

I never touched his baseball card!

I wouldn't have touched anything which he had touched even if you had paid me!

Even any of the sand which he touched—even when it was the sand which he had put in his pail and then gone ahead and dumped it out on the grass—I wouldn't have touched anything that he had been anywhere near—even sand, even that sand, even the sand which he dumped out of his pail on the grass—even when she said if somebody didn't go get it back up and get it back in, even when she said that if somebody didn't, then that she was going to stop the game.

She said, "Pretty is as pretty does."

There was the way it was with his eye, the way it gave you the idea that it was looking straight down, in a straight downward direction, that because of the way his cheek was, the eye just got to look that way, because I know that it really wasn't, that it really couldn't, that if you could just put back what was missing from his cheek, then the eye wouldn't give you that particular impression about which direction it was looking in, that it was just an illusion, or an optical illusion, because it couldn't actually have been looking straight down like that, no eye could have, no eye can look in a straight downward direction, or at least I don't think that any eye can, that any real eye actually can.

Like a peach pit with most of the peach bitten off of it—I can't think of a description which would be better than that one, except for the fact that it was from the hoe, that it was a hoe which did it and not teeth which did.

Also, it was like a trench across, right across almost the very center of the top of his head—so that you could actually hear a squelchy sound every new time when you hit it now.

The water.

The rubberbands.

Him, his head.

And I was probably going something like, "It's a hoe," "It's a toe," and so on and so forth.

You know.

Think back.

You thought you could start anywhere, start with anything, and wouldn't ever have to stop until you'd rhymed them all.

Or choked.

You know what?

He was just as interested in watching as I was.

It was like he wanted to lie back but also keep himself up enough on one elbow to still keep looking up and look.

He said, "Nyou nyon't nyave nyoo nyill nyee."

He said, "Nyou nyidn't nyave nyoo nyill nyee."

But in all reality, he didn't mind.

He probably only really minded it when it was after the hoe part had broken off and it was just the stick itself.

You don't understand.

I myself didn't.

Not until I saw them on the roof.

It took me forty-four years to see it again—and you know what? Now I'll bet, I'll bet that now I'll see nothing else.

Here's another thing which I have been saving up—

namely, the fact that he made a sound that sounded like a greeting when I first gave him that very first one and before he actually fell over from it. What I am saying is that he actually made a sound like this—like "Ahhh"— like something which sounded to me like this was something which he had been waiting for for a long time, and now that it was finally here, he was greeting it, saying hello to it.

I heard him go, "Ahhh."

Only it wasn't really "Ahhh" but "Nyahhh."

In the case of me, however, when I myself got clunked, in this case not by a toy hoe but by the top of a trunk, by the lid of an automobile trunk, of the taxi-cab's trunk, I don't think I made a sound so much as just thought to myself that my knees had just buckled, that for the first time in my life I had actually felt them buckle.

But then I looked down at my knees to see what buckling knees would look like, and when I did that, when I bent over and did that, guess what.

I saw the blood come dropping down in what looked to me like almost like a spout of it—and that's when I screamed, I screamed—when I saw it drop like a long spill of it like that, like it had been in a pail up on top of my head and the pail had tipped a bit and a long splash of it was spilling out, when I saw the first long splash of it go past my eyes in one long stream of it and then splash the street and splash my shoes—I screamed, I screamed—I screamed, "Jesus Christ, I'm killed!"

You don't understand the situation yet, you don't understand—because it wasn't just a question of getting myself whacked in the head like that, it was also a question of a million other things—for instance, what about the footlocker and the duffel bag?

Or of Henry not getting on the bus?

Or even just coming back down and seeing my head?

She was on the stairs.

Then she went back up and got a wet washcloth and then she came back down with it and just sat down and then fell down like sticks.

She was on the stairs when I came in the door.

With shoes and socks on? Without shoes and socks on?

I don't know.

I am not ever going to know.

You don't understand yet, you don't understand yet—Henry and I had taken the footlocker down and taken the duffel bag down and then he himself had gone back up to tell Florence to hurry up while she was getting the rest of her face on and I myself was down in the street still trying to get a cab.

I want you to know something.

I want to admit to you something.

I didn't want the doorman doing it because is **it** worth fifty cents, plus whatever else you'd have to hand over to him for helping you get the footlocker in and the duffel bag in?

When help wouldn't even have been necessary?

But do you think that you could say to the man that you didn't want any help, didn't need any help?

This is the reason why I was up at the corner of Ninety-first and Fifth and not right in front of the building. This is the reason why I was up there with my head split open and with the footlocker in the trunk and the duffel bag on the sidewalk and the cabbie and me both running up and down and not knowing what the next logical move was. In other words, do I let him drive me up to Mount Sinai to the emergency room and there-fore, as far as Henry and Florence are concerned, do I just vanish? Or do I wait there in the street and bleed to death? And if I wait, then won't Henry come down and have to see me with my head wide open? But if I don't wait, then what happens to his things? Do I just leave them there in the street?

Those were nothing.

There were even more questions than those.

Namely, for instance, the biggest one—which is Henry and camp, Henry and camp—what happens if Henry doesn't get there in time to get on the bus to camp, what will Henry do about that?

But then in the middle of all that, then with all of that going on, what do I do next?

It's fantastic, it's really fantastic—I let him slam the door, I work it out so that a door gets slammed right on the ends of these two fingers. Can you imagine?

You should have seen that jacket. You should have seen that sport jacket. You never saw anything like it— and I want you to know something—that morning, the morning of, that was the first time I'd put it on aside from when I was picking it up at Dunhill's and put it on to check on the job they did on it altering it.

And the necktie—never worn before, purchased for just that morning, purchased just for the morning of, and both a total loss, not a thing to be done for either one of them, sopping wet, drenched through and through, a waste, a wreck, a total mess, make no mistake of it, believe you me, the both of them, through and through.

On the television, on the roof, you know what they were wearing—not the shooters, of course, not the men shooting, but the ones who were getting stabbed and were stabbing, those two or three of them?

Like pajamas—like white pajamas.

Like big loose white pajamas.

So that whenever bullets hit them, it looked like raindrops were hitting them—the way the white popped up, little pops of it.

Except our television, it's not a color one, it's a

portable and just a black-and-white one, so that maybe they were just light-colored pajamas and not actually white ones.

But they couldn't have been pajamas. They were just something that had big loose tops and bottoms.

I think I said, "Don't look." I think I just automatically said it.

But I don't know.

I don't remember anything of what I said after I first saw it, after I first looked up from packing Henry's footlocker up and saw it. I don't remember anything of what I did or didn't say to Florence about it. Going to the telephone and calling the station, I remember what I said to the girl who answered the phone for the station, the girl who was the station's nighttime operator, but that's as far as that goes. I mean afterwards, when we went back to finishing the packing and then finally actually went to bed, I don't think I said anything about it, unless I am just automatically forgetting that I did.

In all truthfulness, I think if I said anything, it was probably like something to try to make a joke of it, like something crazy enough to just make a joke out of it—like "Thank God Henry's camp's north of South America"—something jokey like that, I think, so that we could stop thinking about it or just go to sleep and just be free of it.

But maybe I really didn't even speak.

Maybe I still felt like I was in on a secret and didn't want to share and share alike with it.

Don't ask me how, but I tell you that you could just tell that it was on a roof, that it was a roof which you were looking at, that all of them were on the same roof, the two men, or the three men—namely, the men who were getting stabbed and were stabbing, plus the men who had the little machine guns and were shooting them, who were shooting the men who weren't paying any attention to them because they were so busy lying down and getting up and then switching around and going through this same whole funny routine all over again, this thing of getting stabbed by each other and sometimes sort of waking up and stabbing back for a little bit, stabbing back for a little while, and then lying right back down again and looking back up and watching for the other one to take the next turn, waiting for the other one to get up and take the next turn, and neither one of them, or not any of the three of them if there were in fact three of them, neither one of them paying even the slightest attention to all of the bullets that keep going into them, that you can see actually going into them on account of the little pop each bullet makes, all the little puffs they make, in the big loose pajamas which the prisoners have on, just like raindrops, just like raindrops.

Unless I'm wrong to call them the prisoners.

I really don't know who was what—except that two of them had little machine guns and two had knives—or three, three had knives, the three men in the pajamas—if it actually just wasn't that I only thought I saw a third one.

Not that I don't realize that some of this probably just has to be my imagination filling things in for me, not that some of this maybe wasn't more or less imagined on the spot or just automatically thought up afterwards, or more or less seen at the time with all sorts of tiny little inaccuracies in it, little things not seen too clearly at the time, not seen so clearly at the time because let's remember the particular circumstances—the hour of the night, the physical exhaustion, plus the fact that I just looked up and there it was without any warning, that the thing was already going on and no one had ever even given me the least warning, the volume off and no announcer and no explanation, and make no mistake of it, our screen is not all that big in the first place, it is actually a fairly small screen, a fairly small television, since there is absolutely, but absolutely no point at all in your always just having to fork over for the kind of repair costs which they just love to smack you with when you come to them with one of those big extravagant ones broken, with one of those extravagant big ones.

When I say pops, puffs, what I mean is like with

sand, like with sand—that's the perfect example for what I mean, of what I meant—it raining on sand is—like raindrops first hitting what's totally dry sand—that's just what it looked like, what the bullets hitting them looked like, making those puffs in their clothes, those tops and bottoms popping up in places, those things like pajamas which the two of them had on, which the two of them or the three of them had on.

I saw it sometimes, rain first starting up on the sand in the sandbox. But mostly the little roof kept it off of it, the little fringed awning thing which went over the top of Andy Lieblich's sandbox.

I take it back about the fringe. I cannot swear to the fringe.

But it's all the difference, you know—the fringe. A little thing like just fringe, it can make all the difference—or a thing even littler than fringe can.

You know what?

The littler it is, the bigger the difference which it can make. Maybe not right off the bat, but give it time, give it time.

I don't want you to miss this—a dozen times a day I'll feel for a granule under a fingernail.

Here's a laugh for you—namely, that I didn't even lose them—the fingernails on those two fingers, I can't even say that I lost the fingernail on either one of those two fingers—I can't even claim that there was that much damage.

There wasn't any damage.

You know what the most damage was?

Having to still remember how it felt when I first felt it—the air there, air which was where there hadn't been any air before, air which is actually inside of you, which gets inside of you, or which gets to you where you yourself have been turned inside out.

The reason why I say it was a roof, what convinced me, the things which gave it the look of a roof to me, which made it look that way to me even though it was a flat place, even though what the man with the television camera was taking a picture of was just a big-looking flat place, were things like this—things like flues and funnels, if that's what you call them, all those different kinds of chimney things, those big exhaust things, which they always have up on the roofs of big buildings—those like different shapes of vent things that stick up and turn around sometimes, revolve sometimes, or have like hats on them, like what looks like Chinese hats on top of them, or ribbed things, like ribbed crownlike sheet-metal things which turn around from something, which revolve or spin around from the wind or from exhaust or something mechanical moving.

I tell you, it looked like the roof of what she said it was.

It looked like the roof of a prison.

Or at least it looked like the roof of a big building.

I say a big one because of all these big sheet-metal things which were sticking up from the top of it—funnels, flues, whatever.

Think of words like dredge, like carborundum, like drogue, like torque—because that's what, those are just what it looked like, like every single solitary one of those.

That's it.

That's all.

The man with the camera never moved the camera even once, not even once, that I myself saw. He just kept it pinned, he just kept it stationed in the same place—namely, centered on the two men, or if it was really three men, then on the three men who were in the pajamas and who were being stabbed by each other and who were stabbing each other while there were these two other men who were meanwhile shooting them with little machine guns, whereas those two men, the two men with machine guns, as for them insofar as the picture itself goes, they were both on one side of it, you could see them both there on the same side of it, which was actually over at the very edge of it over on one side.

What I mean is this—that just the way the man

with the camera didn't move the camera, that just the way he kept the camera so totally stuck there in the one place and didn't even shift it around any to show you anything close up or anything else in the center of the picture instead, just the way he didn't move it for a little bit even to show you, for instance, the men with the little machine guns centered in the middle of the picture—just that alone, just the dead weight of the camera alone, just that in and of itself alone made the whole thing all that much more of something which you yourself could not look away from, either—which you had to look at the same way the man who was taking the picture was.

I mean, it made you like the man with the camera—it's true, it's true, I couldn't move.

Did I tell you that they were acting like they didn't even notice?

That the ones who were getting shot, did I tell you that they were getting shot all over, but that you would never have known it, that you would never have known it, that the only way you could tell wasn't from their faces but was from the pops, the pops, the little puffs?

Maybe the third man had a length of something—not a knife in itself, not a knife as such, but just a length of something—something which it just looked like he was stabbing with but he really wasn't.

If there was a third man.

Peruvian police, Peruvian policemen—the men with the little machine guns must have been Peruvian policemen.

I never saw people get killed so much.

But it didn't make any difference to the people who were getting it. They were only interested in the stabbing part. All they were paying attention to was whose turn it was, who went next, who got to lie down and look up and see how it looked.

Which was all that he himself was interested in, either—namely, which the cameraman was.

Homespun—you think that that's what those tops and bottoms could have been made out of?

But in all honesty and sincerity, I cannot say that I felt the rake.

I'll tell you what I can say.

I can say that I felt the hoe more than I felt the rake!

Even when we were both turning in different directions and pulling away, him up and me down, even then I still didn't feel it all that much.

Or as much.

You could almost say that Kobbe Koffi and I, that we were a team like that—him down and me up or whatever—what with Henry on his way back upstairs to get Florence to hurry up, what with Henry not there to help me get it up. I mean, the man could not have been more helpful—the driver, the cab driver—you couldn't be killed by a nicer man.

Just imagine it, just imagine it—what if I hadn't sent Henry back up, just suppose Henry had not gone back up to tell Florence to get a move on, what if he had been right there in the street, what if he'd seen the whole thing when I leaned back in, when I leaned back in so that I could reach far enough back in to snatch the little snippet of whatever off, suppose Henry had been right there when the whole thing had happened, when I leaned back in to get that little snippet of something off, yank off whatever it was that was stuck onto the top of the footlocker—I mean, you look up and there's your father, there is your father, with his head like that, with blood like that, with blood just dropping out of it like something out of a pail.

Think of it, think of it—being seen by your son like that.

You feel a chill, you know.

Even on a hot day like that was, you feel a chill when the air first gets to it—namely, to a place where you are not used to feeling it.

I think part of why you like it when you're looking up is just the air part. I think it makes you feel more like there's nothing there but gossamer—that the chill which you feel does.

It was just before you got to the hairline actually.

That was probably the worst of it—pulling off the Band-Aid from where some hair had gotten caught under it, pulling off the Band-Aid when the whole thing was all better, which was maybe all of two or three days later.

Incredible.

I would have bet money on it, I would actually have been willing to bet money on it that I wouldn't have even made it up to Mount Sinai, that I wouldn't have even lived to make it the ten, twelve blocks back uptown to Mount Sinai, whereas two, three days later what am I doing but pulling off a Band-Aid off my forehead—and you know what? By that time, by the time I was getting rid of that one, I didn't even have the two other ones on me anymore, the two Band-Aids that they had put on me for where I'd mashed my fingers—or actually just pinched them, just gotten them pinched in the door actually.

But he thought he'd killed me, too.

I think that the fact is this—that we were both of us shrieking.

You know what the question was?

It was this—what is the next thing to do?

They weren't even special Band-Aids. They were just the kind which anybody can get just from walking into any drugstore or dimestore or supermarket.

Some persons might regard a ninth of a mile as a great distance. But distances are relative. Everything is relative—everything but the one thing which we all of us know isn't.

And wasn't.

That's the thing—wasn't!

Wait for them to come down and bleed to death? Or just go with Kobbe Koffi?

She just went up and she just came down—and then she sat down on the floor and didn't do anything.

Here's what happened—we lifted the footlocker up together and we got it into the trunk together and then I went to lean back in to get something off the top of the footlocker while he was slamming down the lid of the trunk.

That's what happened, plain and simple.

It was probably just a piece of whatever kind of tape it was which Florence was using to get the inventory to stick on inside up inside of the footlocker.

Whereas in the case of the duffel bag, it was threads. It was some threads. It was from reaching back into the back seat to yank off some threads where they were left over from sewing up the seam.

I tell you, all that was missing was the top hat and the cane.

And the banana peel.

Mothers out with toddlers, fathers on the way to their offices, kids waiting for day-camp vans—they all just looked at me, they all just looked—a man screaming like a crazy man and running all around.

You know what they probably thought?

They probably thought that he'd done it to me—the colored man. I mean, the driver.

Actually, he did do it to me.

Airducts.

I think you call some of those things airducts. But whether they take the air in or the air out, I for one do not know, I for one could not say.

It was all just seconds, really—it was all just a question of seconds. And I think I should mention another aspect to it, another aspect of it, which was from the billowiness of the tops and bottoms—namely, that there was a clown aspect to it, like an act being put on by clowns—toy knives and rubber bulbs in their pockets so that when they go ahead and squeeze them you see these little puffs all over their clothes.

They really had long knives.

Whereas the third man, he might have just had a length of something else.

But you couldn't really tell if he existed or not, if whether you were looking at two men or at three men, or even if whether they were prisoners and hostages or whatever—but I think that that was actually because I didn't completely know what it all was until after, until later, until the girl finally told me Peru.

Here's why you couldn't count.

The funnels and whatever, one or two of the men was always, or were always, coming out from behind one of those big vents or big funnels.

Those airducts.

They came out and did some stabbing and then they lay down to get stabbed and then they got up and went back behind the funnel or whatever.

Maybe they went back behind there to get away from the bullets.

You couldn't really count them, say for a certain two or three of them.

Florence called it out and I wrote it down—so many this, so many that.

I'm going to tell you something. When he gets home,

when he gets home—judging from summers past, we're lucky if even half of it comes home with him!

There is something else that you should know—namely, that I think you should know that there wasn't really any way to get all of that sand back up into the sandbox once you'd actually gone ahead and dumped it out of it.

I can see it now, all right—the humor of it, the comedy of it, a fellow all dressed up like that—blam, blam—ouch, ouch—top hat, banana peel, cane!

Those men on the roof, they'd be doing it in Spanish, wouldn't they?

I mean, if that's what they actually speak in Peru.

They'd be going something like "Funnel," "Tunnel," "Munnel."

And so on and so forth.

Except in Spanish, if that's their poison.

It was in fact, there is absolutely, but absolutely no question of it, the plain and simple fact is that it was a meatloaf sandwich, that my mother never gave me bologna.

And a chocolate drink, not soda.

He actually said, "Nyahhh."

As if in greeting, as if in acknowledgment.

Think of it, think of it—only six years old and already ready for it, ready and waiting for it.

I felt like a silly goon, like a total goon, out there in the middle of everything, my knees buckling like some total clown—but the other thing was this.

That I felt like I was his lady-in-waiting.

Kobbe Koffi's.

Not that I knew his name just then—I didn't know his name until I finally decided to get inside of the taxi and let Kobbe Koffi save my life.

Here's one for you!

Where's Togoland?

You think I went and found out where Togoland is? I've had since June, since July—and now it's what? It's August, it's August, it's almost the twenty-first of August—but you think I've gone ahead and looked it up?

I know where Peru is.

Listen to this, this is one of the best things which I've been saving up, this is one of the best things of all the things which have to do with all of this—imagine me bleeding more from what happened to me than he did from all of that—a whole trench across the top of his head, a whole split-apart trench, and his cheek, his cheek like what it looks like when you're eating a peach and you're down to the pit.

I said, "A place for everything, and everything in its place." Or maybe I just thought it. But he couldn't get it back in. You would have to be really good at things to get it back in. I probably could have, but was it my job to? Maybe it was my job to do it for Andy Lieblich if he himself had spilled it out. However, I don't think that you could say that it was my specific job to just go ahead and do it for just anybody who came along in general, but I think that he in particular thought so. I think that something had given him the idea that because I was the one who had to wait outside, then that it just automatically meant that it was my specific job to be the one who had to put things back, who had to always be the one to put everything back.

Maybe one of them was going like this—"Airduct," "Airduck."

In the language of Peru.

But make no mistake of it, I don't mean that it would be the words themselves which would be in that language—I just mean that the idea of the thing would be.

Believe you me, the words are never the point.

I couldn't believe it, I couldn't believe it—when I finally just went ahead and made up my mind, I just couldn't believe it when I got inside and looked over the seat and saw his name on the thing which they all have to have up there, I tell you, I just couldn't believe it from the standpoint of the man having such a crazy name, was this going to mean good luck for me or bad?

Even in Togoland it could be a totally crazy name.

You know why she said that it was binding her?

The reason that she said that it was binding her was because she wanted everybody to stop and pay attention to the fact that even if she had to have a son like that, that it still didn't mean that she herself didn't have bigger ones than my own mother did.

You think six years old, you think that when someone is just six years old, do you think that when you are still only just at the age of only six years old that you actually couldn't know anything about a thing which works like that?

It was soggy and squelchy, but there wasn't what you could call that much of it coming out. It was mostly his buttons which had it on them—and some of the sand in the sandbox. But it was nothing in comparison to the way it was the morning of, when it just came dropping out.

I'll tell you how they explained it when I got up to Mount Sinai and they saw that it was just a scratch, just a scrape, underneath. They said that the whole thing of it is just a question of the different amounts of local blood which you have in various places. But I think that it's probably that age has something to do with it, too— that plus the fact that I was running all around like a total maniac, whereas he was mainly lying fairly still.

Except for when he got up for a while and went looking in his pockets and kept asking me to answer the question of "Nyere's Nyonny Nyize?"

I'm no medical expert, of course—but in all honesty and sincerity, I think that you would have to say that he was almost dead by then.

Maybe a dozen times a day—like a little grain of it just pushing up from underneath.

That's probably an exaggeration, that many times of the day.

But I'll tell you this—if you look close enough, it sometimes looks to you like you can still see a bit of the door grease stuck in around the creases and the cuticles.

It's time to confess something—namely, that I don't think I could go ahead and eat a soft-boiled egg if you paid me.

My forehead, just under the hairline, believe you me, even what with it being a hot day like that, the first impression you have is the feeling that you are having a chill on account of the air that gets in there.

That wild Indian of mine, he's due back what? Tomorrow? Tomorrow?

That imp!

That rascal!

I'll bet he'll be twice the size he was when he left here just weeks ago!

What I thought I was doing when I reached my hand back in to the back seat to get those threads off I for one emphatically, but emphatically don't know, can't say, can't even begin to tell you.

I'm telling you, I'm telling you, they heard me up and down the avenue—that was a scream to wake the dead—but what did it all amount to, what with all that carrying on, what did it all come to in the end?

But you know what? In a way, it was fun—the scare, thinking that was it, curtains, etc.

She had long plain bony flat fingers with never any rings on them and never any nail polish on them, and with not even long nails, either, but with just the dust from the chalk on them and with the light that it looked to you like it was coming from down inside of them, from down inside of the bones inside of her fingers.

That's how I saw them when she held the book

and I looked up—I saw the tips of chalky lit-up fingers, the flesh polished and ghostly and glowy and white.

I sat in the very first row and looked up.

She read from the book and I looked up.

What they did on that roof, what they did on that roof—do you have any idea of what they did on that roof?

Why do they do that?

Is everybody a lady-in-waiting?

She said, "See, everybody?"

She turned the book around and said to us, "Can everybody see?"

She said to us, "Boys and girls, do you see?"

It was always something so wonderful, and there, there, there—there was always her finger on it.

Blue Coal wasn't blue. It was just black the way coal was.

One of them would get up and start stabbing back and then the other one would lie back down and watch.

You know what it must be—it must be that everybody's waiting.

"Phil? Phil? Is that you? Is that you?"

How I used to suffer before somebody talked me into going ahead and trying mineral oil!

I'll tell you something—I don't know if they really

had them back then, but I think they did, that they were different and had an oil burner.

I know the day he's coming. I know the time exactly.

That thing about Togoland, that was when we were heading up Madison Avenue to Mount Sinai. Maybe I said, "Kobbe Koffi, that's a new one on me, a name like Kobbe Koffi." Maybe that's what I said, and him, maybe he said, "Be plenty more like it in Togoland."

If that's how it was, then it was probably just a question of saying something by way of trying to pass the time, by way of just making conversation. As I said, like I said, it's not the words—the words are never the thing. It's the situations—it's those and the people which are in them. I mean, look at it this way—wasn't I the one who was making believe that I was dying, and wasn't he the one who had to act like he'd gone and accidentally killed me?

You know.

You just say anything.

Maybe I said, "Just look at this jacket. Can you believe it? I just this morning first put it on. Not even an hour ago, and it's hundreds of dollars."

Maybe I said, "Did you ever try Vernax on a shoe?"

I think I said, "They say that kale gives you red blood."

You know what I think? I think he said Togoland just to help me get my mind off of it. I'm telling you, the man could have been as dumb about Togoland as I am.

If there even is a Togoland.

There is a Peru.

I think I said, "What do you think they'll do when they come down and nothing's there?"

Or maybe I said, "I want a Christian burial. Tell them to give me a Christian burial."

I know I said the craziest things.

I believe I said, "All I wanted was to be presentable."

I know I said this, "Let's pray he makes the bus."

I said, "Please God he makes the bus."

I said, "Lilac, hankie, chamois, bodice."

She used to say, "Gordon, can you say gossamer?"

I said to him, "Go through the light, go through the light—it's an emergency, don't stop, don't stop!"

Not that it really was, of course.

But the man actually stopped when I tell you, I tell you, he could have gone right through!

I kept on screaming it at him—"No!" I kept on screaming it—"Oh, keep on going, *please*!"

I screamed.

Here is what I screamed.

I screamed, "We are on our way out of here and out of all of this shit, this big boogie dickhead and me!"

It was wonderful.

It was so wonderful, the whole feeling of the way everything made you feel how it was going to lift right up from where it was—and then he did it and did it, went through, ran the light, the taxi trembling like it meant to fucking jump.

Then, then—I was the happiest then as I have ever been.

I said, "I remember it, I think."

I said, "If it's an emergency, I mean."

I said, "Isn't it Lackawanna 4-1810?"